Praise for *Change Fluency*

"*Change Fluency* is an essential playbook for leaders who understand that meaningful change isn't about doing more but about focusing deliberately on what matters most."

GREG MCKEOWN, *New York Times*–bestselling author of *Essentialism* and *Effortless*

"A must-read for anyone serious about designing differentiated change. Practical, insightful, and grounded in what actually works."

KAREN BALL, author of *The ADKAR Advantage*

"Innovation without the ability to navigate change is a wasted opportunity. This book bridges that gap brilliantly."

CHRIS BARTON, CEO of Shazam

"Innovation is meaningless without execution, and execution is impossible without mastering change. This book is the ultimate guide to making disruption work for you."

SHAWN KANUNGO, bestselling author of *The Bold Ones*

"If disruption keeps wearing you down, *Change Fluency* is your counterpunch. Jay Kiew delivers brutally honest insights and tactics to transform your change angst into innovation swagger."

DAN PONTEFRACT, award-winning author of *Work-Life Bloom* and *Lead. Care. Win.*

"The future is imagined and shaped by those who embrace change and take action toward more hopeful futures. This book is the essential guide to developing the ability to remain flexible and have fluency ahead of the unknown world ahead of us."

NIKOLAS BADMINTON, chief futurist and hope engineer of Futurist.com

"Forget everything you think you know about change management. *Change Fluency* rewires how you think, lead, and create. It reads like a thriller, teaches like a master class, and delivers insights that will revolutionize your approach to innovation. Bold, clear, and essential for any leader who refuses to let innovation remain a buzzword."

JOSH LINKNER, three-time *New York Times*–bestselling author of *Big Little Breakthroughs, Disciplined Dreaming*, and *The Road to Reinvention*

"*Change Fluency* is the road map we all wish we had when navigating messy, uncertain systems. Jay Kiew translates the unspoken rules of change into clear, actionable principles that help you lead, adapt, and stand out—no matter your title."

GORICK NG, *Wall Street Journal*–bestselling author of *The Unspoken Rules*

"Change is relational. Jay Kiew brilliantly captures how deep change requires not just bold ideas but brave conversations and authentic connection."

CHRIS SCHEMBRA, *Wall Street Journal*–bestselling author of *Gratitude Through Hard Times*

"Change these days is less a path and more a wave. To succeed, you have to be water. This book offers insights and strategies to be fluent and fluid—and succeed in change."

MICHAEL BUNGAY STANIER, *Wall Street Journal*–bestselling author of *The Coaching Habit* and founder of Change Signal

"Jay empowers us to champion innovative change at work by meaningfully connecting with purpose, people and positive disruption."

RIAZ MEGHJI, author of *Every Conversation Counts*

Change Fluency

9 Principles to Navigate Uncertainty and Drive Innovation

Jay Kiew

Change
Fluency

PAGE TWO

Cataloguing in publication information is
available from Library and Archives Canada.
ISBN 978-1-77458-699-0 (paperback)
ISBN 978-1-77458-700-3 (ebook)

Page Two
pagetwo.com

Page Two™ is a trademark owned by
Page Two Strategies Inc., and is used under
license by authorized licensees

Cover and interior design by Cameron McKague
Interior illustrations by Justin De Leon

changefluency.com

Contents

Preface

Across the Airwaves: Disruption of an Industry

The soft hum of radio static filled the radio station in Singapore as my father, Roger Kool, adjusted the dials on his TASCAM recorder. It didn't occur to me that a blind DJ navigating a mixer with ease was unusual. It was 1994, and at age five, I was already accustomed to the red On Air sign's rhythm—blinking at me to stay quiet and retreat to my corner with a book, then disappearing, which gave me permission to run in and join my dad in the studio. The booth was my second home, a window to an industry on the brink of transformation.

My parents, Roger Kool and Lynette Loon, were radio DJs throughout the '70s, '80s, and '90s. This gave me a front-row seat to disruption in its purest form.

They worked for various radio stations across Singapore and Sri Lanka—Rediffusion, Heart 91.3, Yes.FM—playing the latest Top 40 music during the night slot and over the weekends. I watched as celebrity musicians came through for interviews, my parents chatting with the greats of the '90s era, from Boyz II Men to Britney Spears. They would recount seemingly unreal stories of conversations with Toni Braxton, Stevie Wonder, Michael Jackson... each interaction a snapshot of an industry at its peak.

But as I grew up, things changed. The transformation wasn't just subtle shifts; it was seismic upheavals, one after the other.

The Death of the TASCAM Tape

I remember the exact moment I realized everything was about to change. It was the early '90s and my father was in the booth, carefully handling a TASCAM tape, his fingers moving with the precision of a surgeon.

For a DJ, a TASCAM tape was like a wand for a wizard, a mini recording studio in his hands. Picture a compact cassette tape onto which you could squeeze eight tracks into one. Before we were able to digitally mix sound seamlessly, these tapes were revolutionary, allowing radio DJs to record and mix songs, voices, sound effects, background music, and jingles—all without recording one track over another.

These tapes were the lifeblood of radio, containing not only music but the sponsored hour-long sessions that paid our bills. Companies like Coca-Cola would sponsor Dad's sets for large department stores like Isetan. He would curate the music, pausing every few songs to thank shoppers for stopping by, shouting out the latest Coke flavor available in their food court.

"This is the last TASCAM recorder in Singapore," my father told me one evening, his voice carrying a weight I hadn't heard before. "The supplier isn't making them anymore. Everyone's moving to digital."

I watched him handle that tape with extra care that night, knowing it represented more than just technology. It was the end of an era. The physical connection between DJ and audience, the tangible craft of radio production, was slipping away.

The transformation was relentless.

TASCAM tapes and vinyl records gave way to cassettes and CDs. Those quickly disappeared as MP3s brought music into the virtual realm. By the time I left university, MP3s had been replaced by streaming, and radio stations had become something you listened to on your commute if you had no other choice: Who would choose random songs with irritating ads over a seamlessly curated Spotify playlist powered by billions of data points?

As the demand for traditional radio faded, my parents, burned out from the late hours and constant adaptation, began looking for somewhere to build a better life.

My family moved. A lot.

Change became part of my DNA: eight moves before I turned twelve, from Singapore to Edmonton, from Colombo to Vancouver. With each move came a new elementary school, a new environment, a new language, a new group of strangers among whom I had to find friends.

The choice was apparent: Adapt or be lonely and friendless for the semester.

What Could We Become?

The TASCAM recorder sat silent in my father's radio booth that final evening, a relic of an era about to end. But what I remember most isn't the technology's death knell—it's what happened the next morning. Instead of mourning the old ways, my father gathered his team and asked a simple question: "What could radio become?"

That question led to a mindset shift for me from *what is* to *what could be*. It has shaped my entire approach to transformation. After witnessing my parents navigate the disruption of radio, I've spent the last two decades as an innovation strategist helping organizations drive over $2 billion in transformational impact. From $18-million enterprise resource planning (ERP) implementations to $150-million health care policy reforms, each project has taught me something crucial: The greatest barrier to transformation isn't technological—it's *psychological*.

Yet most organizations still treat change like a mechanical upgrade: systems to implement, processes to optimize, metrics to track. I witnessed this recently at a global tech company where leadership had mapped every technical aspect of their digital transformation. Their diagrams were perfect, their timelines precise. But they'd overlooked something fundamental: Transformation isn't about changing what we do—it's about evolving *how we think* about what we do.

You might wonder how a story about radio DJs in the 1990s connects to your current challenges this year. The truth is the fundamentals of disruption haven't changed; only the pace has accelerated. The same forces that transformed the radio industry are at work in your organization today:

- technology evolving faster than teams can adapt

- customer expectations shifting overnight

- new competitors emerging from unexpected directions

- traditional revenue models becoming obsolete

Change can't
be managed;
**it's a skill that
we must become
fluent in.**

My journey from watching my father navigate the death of analog radio to helping organizations drive billions in transformation impact has taught me something crucial: The technical challenges of change haven't shifted much, but our approach to the human side of transformation must evolve.

After all, as I reflect on the music industry, it didn't die with radio; it simply shifted to a different medium. The transformation of the music industry from radio to YouTube and Spotify has allowed countless artists to find their voices and rack up billions of listens, and now a record label is no longer a necessity but a nice-to-have.

And as for my parents? Well, they adapted as the music industry did, finding new ways to get creative, and ultimately started a production company that flourished by leveraging the latest in technology. They became change fluent.

Who This Book Is For

Change Fluency is written for leaders at every level: whether you're guiding a team, driving a program, or shepherding an entire organization through change. Perhaps you're struggling to navigate transformation and innovation has become both essential and elusive.

You might be

- a product or technology leader trying to differentiate in a rapidly converging market,

- a senior executive facing competitive disruption from unexpected directions,

- a mid-level manager tasked with driving innovation while maintaining existing operations, or

- a team leader seeking to energize your people despite constant change.

You're grappling with questions like

- "How do we create meaningful differentiation when everyone has access to the same tools and technology?"

- "What's the secret to bringing teams along during transformation without burning them out?"

- "How do we innovate when we're consumed by maintaining what we've already built?"

- "How do we lead others through uncertainty when we're still finding our own way?"

Consider the changes over the past few years, in which we have seen pandemics, economic shifts, trade wars, pace of technology, environmental pressures, social and political movements—and we haven't even begun to consider the organizational ones.

I don't believe that change can be *managed*; it's a skill that we must become *fluent* in.

What Is Change Fluency™?

Change Fluency™ is the adaptive capacity for individuals and organizations to navigate uncertainty with confidence and connection. The Change Fluency model is the deliberate development of an organization's capacity to *discover what's possible, design the future,* and *differentiate from the standard.*

Think of it like learning a new language. At first, every interaction is deliberate, even uncomfortable. You translate each word mentally before speaking. But with practice, the language becomes part of you. You develop "muscle memory" that allows you to express complex ideas without conscious effort. Change Fluency works the same way. Through deliberate practice, you build the capacity to adapt, evolve, and innovate despite—or because of—constant disruption.

Unlike traditional change management, which attempts to control outcomes, Change Fluency builds the capacity to thrive within uncertainty while bringing others along. It cultivates both the personal confidence to face the unknown and the relational skills to create meaningful connection throughout transformation.

The most effective leaders don't just manage change; they embody fluency across *three* categories and *nine* dimensions, setting up the structure of this book.

Categories of Change Fluency

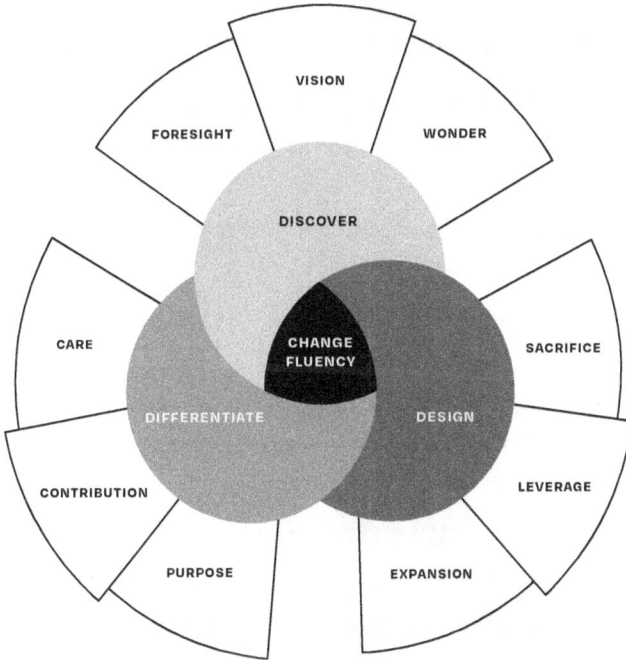

Part 1: Discover What's Possible

Foresight: They recognize patterns in seemingly chaotic environments to imagine more desirable futures.

Vision: They evolve vision through collaboration rather than by mandating it.

Wonder: They embrace wonder rather than demanding certainty.

Part 2: Design the Future

Sacrifice: They make strategic sacrifices instead of adding complexity.

Leverage: They transform constraints into competitive advantages.

Expansion: They create new market possibilities rather than competing in existing ones.

Part 3: Differentiate from the Standard

Purpose: They connect organizational purpose to personal meaning.

Contribution: They cultivate genuine contribution rather than mere participation.

Care: They create with authentic care even at scale.

Like fluency in a new language, Change Fluency develops through practice, grows stronger with application, and ultimately transforms how you experience and shape the world around you.

What's at Stake Without Change Fluency?

Without developing Change Fluency, the stakes are both immediate and far-reaching, affecting individuals, teams, and entire organizations.

For *individuals*, the absence of Change Fluency means career stagnation as skills and mindsets become obsolete in rapidly evolving industries. Decision paralysis becomes common, with people freezing in uncertainty or making fear-based choices rather than strategic ones. The resulting chronic stress creates a cycle where each new disruption feels increasingly overwhelming, leading to burnout and disengagement.

For *teams*, the cost is measured in initiative fatigue— that collective eye-rolling when yet another transformation is announced. Without Change Fluency, your most adaptable team members inevitably leave for organizations where innovation is valued and supported. Those who remain develop a form of organizational learned helplessness, where the effort to champion change no longer feels worthwhile.

For *organizations*, the stakes become existential. Like the radio industry transformation my parents witnessed, entire business models can become obsolete when organizations lack the fluency to evolve with changing customer needs. The innovation drought that follows creates a widening gap between organizational capability and market reality—a gap competitors are all too eager to fill.

What makes a lack of Change Fluency particularly dangerous is the compounding effect. Each failed change initiative reinforces resistance to future changes, making the organization progressively less adaptable over time. Meanwhile, the rate of change in the external environment continues to accelerate, creating a widening chasm between what's possible and what your organization can deliver.

This is precisely what happened to Artemis, a fictional tech company, in the story you're about to read. The gap between its Change Fluency and the market's evolution created an extinction-level crisis that threatened everything it had built. Without developing the Change Fluency principles you'll discover in these pages, organizations like Artemis face not just temporary setbacks but permanent obsolescence.

In a world where disruption is inevitable, Change Fluency isn't just a competitive advantage; it's a survival requirement.

Our greatest innovation isn't what we create **but in how we create it *together*.**

What You Can Expect

In writing this book, I wanted to freely draw on the lessons I've learned from some of the biggest transformations I've tackled over my career, such as

- leading large-scale financial transformations, including an $18-million ERP implementation and running a $100-million portfolio of digital health products;

- driving significant policy and organizational change through a $150-million health care policy reform and restructuring a seventy-five-person team;

- integrating acquisitions and technologies, including purchasing a $30-million business and successfully merging their people, processes, and systems;

- implementing strategic AI and digital transformation initiatives across industries from construction to financial services;

- scaling businesses rapidly and growing a company 4x from small cap (under $2B) to mid-cap ($2B+) in just two years;

- accelerating product growth and user adoption, doubling app users from one million to two million, and scaling fifteen product lines to $35 million in twelve months; and

- developing market expansion strategies that helped companies reach $100-million milestones and create entirely new market opportunities.

It felt like the ultimate challenge: How could I synthesize what I've learned over the past two decades about the inter-weaving of change management, enterprise strategy, and innovation? Having worked with over four hundred executives across industries, it felt like there were endless stories that I could tell.

I found myself imagining the world in the near future. *What would our world look like? What would our futures for work look like? Would we still face as many disruptions as we do now? What would leadership mean in those moments?*

I found myself sketching out a futuristic fable that tells the story of Lee, VP of Product at Artemis, a massive tech company facing disruption after disruption. Set in 2035, this story captures the core insights from my organizational transformations, as well as what I wish leaders would practice to bring their teams along on the journey.

Throughout each chapter, you'll find

- Lee's ongoing story, which serves as a narrative thread demonstrating how these principles play out in practice;

- From the Field, real-world case studies and examples that bring concepts to life; and

- Put It into Practice, practical exercises you can implement immediately.

The book follows the Change Fluency framework through three core sections:

Part 1: Discover What's Possible (chapters 1–8) explores the fundamental barriers to change—the five chains that hold organizations back: Clutter and Chaos, Comfort with the Status Quo, Competing Interests, Constraints, and Apathy. In these chapters, you'll gain a road map to assess where your transformation initiative may be stuck and discover the first three innovation principles: Zoom Out to Zoom In, Evolve Your Vision, and Work in Wonder.

Part 2: Design the Future (chapters 9–11) reveals how to turn constraints into catalysts and vision into velocity through three powerful innovation principles: Strategy Is Sacrifice, Leverage Your Limits, and Paint a Bigger Canvas. These chapters provide practical approaches to designing change that sticks.

Part 3: Differentiate from the Standard (chapters 12–14) shows how to make your transformation stand out through the final three innovation principles: Make Your Mission Personal, Cultivate Contribution over Participation, and Create with Care. These chapters help you move beyond standard approaches to create truly distinctive change.

In chapter 1, you'll meet Lee, a tech leader whose company faces extinction-level disruption when its competitor gains three hundred million users in a single week. Through Lee's journey, which is built on my innovation experience partnering with four hundred executives over the past fifteen years—and through real-world examples from Nintendo to Costco, from lululemon to Toyota—you'll discover how organizations create meaningful differentiation in a world where traditional competitive advantages disappear overnight.

Welcome to the age of intelligence, where our greatest innovation isn't what we create but in how we create it *together*.

PART ONE

DISCOVER WHAT'S POSSIBLE

1
Man on Fire

Reality Check in a Robotaxi

The Seattle skyline pierced through the morning fog, its
familiar silhouette a reminder of why Lee had chosen
to build his life here, just like his father had three decades
ago. The world might see Seattle as Microsoft's backyard
or Amazon's playground, but for Lee, it was where the
impossible happened—where immigrant dreams took root
in rain-soaked soil and grew into tech giants.

Lee stared at the notification lighting up his phone's
display.

He couldn't believe what he was seeing.

Three hundred million users. Within a week of
launching.

His hand trembled slightly as he refreshed Delta Tech's
statistics again, each new number burning into his con-
sciousness. Delta, Artemis' biggest competitor, wasn't just
winning, it was obliterating the market landscape Lee had
known for a decade.

As VP of Product for Artemis' flagship AI division,
he'd seen his share of concerning metrics, but this was
different.

Through the robotaxi's smart windows, he watched the
city scroll past—the same route he'd taken for eight years,

from his home in Queen Anne to Artemis' campus in South
Lake Union. The environmental display shimmered, transforming the window into a gentle data visualization of their
carbon-neutral journey through the tech corridor.

Eight years at Artemis, the last six months heading
its most crucial division, and now this. His team of two
hundred engineers and researchers had trusted his vision,
followed his methodical approach to building the future of
work collaboration: AI systems that could anticipate needs,
streamline communications, and make remote work feel
more human. They'd believed in his promise of responsible innovation. Now, in 2035, Delta had made their careful
progress look like cautious baby steps, and those same team
members would be looking to him for answers he wasn't
sure he had.

The familiar landmarks scrolled past: the Space Needle piercing the fog, Lake Union's waters chopped by early
morning seaplanes, and finally the gleaming Artemis campus—all of it feeling suddenly fragile.

"Your heart rate appears elevated," the taxi's AI noted, its
Pacific Northwest vocal setting matching Lee's own accent.
"Would you like me to play some calming music for the
remainder of your journey? Or perhaps you'd like to review
a pleasant memory?"

*This taxi's AI is more emotionally intelligent than most of my
engineering team*, Lee thought.

Teleported to the Past

Before Lee could decline, his phone's neural interface
flickered to life, projecting a holographic snippet from three
months ago—his daughter Grace's science fair at Roosevelt
Elementary. The scene played out in crystalline detail:

gymnasium lights reflecting off a crude but earnest neural network designed to recognize dog breeds, Grace's face beaming with pride next to her blue ribbon.

"See, Dad? It only gets it right about 60 percent of the time right now," Grace's voice echoed through the memory. "But that's okay because even AIs have to learn and grow, right? Just like you always say about your teams at Artemis!"

The other parents had gathered around, drawn by Grace's infectious excitement about artificial intelligence, a subject that, until recently, had been Artemis' undisputed territory in the competitive tech landscape.

"Your dad must be teaching you all about AI," one of the parents had said, looking at Lee with that familiar mix of respect and subtle envy that came with his position at Artemis. "You're lucky to have an insider track on the future!"

Grace had straightened up then, pride radiating from every inch of her four-foot-nine frame. "Dad's company makes the best AI in the world! He says that by the time I'm ready, artificial intelligence will be as normal as electricity. And he promised that someday, there'll be a place for me at Artemis where I can help make it even better!"

Maybe it's not that bad? Lee thought, his typical West Coast optimism struggling against hard reality. *After all, we at Artemis have 320 million global customers on our work collaboration platform.* His division's AI features were being used by some of the biggest companies in the world. They'd won awards for their responsible innovation approach.

The thought died as quickly as it formed. *No, dummy, that took a decade to build. And Delta did that in a week. It's a big fucking problem.*

His phone buzzed with a message from Teresa, his wife: "Grace asking if you can help with AI homework tonight. Says she wants to 'train her model like they do at Artemis.' You up for it?"

The words blurred as Lee's mind drifted to the small wooden box sitting on his desk at home, containing his father's old developer badge from Microsoft—scratched, faded, but still bearing the proud smile of a man who had left Singapore for Seattle's promise of technological revolution.

His father's words echoed in Lee's mind: "Innovation isn't inherited, Lee. Since it's inevitable that every generation will see its disruptions, our success is determined by our ability to become fluent with *any* change. Adapt or die."

The stark finality of those last three words hit Lee differently now. His father hadn't just been sharing wisdom; he'd been passing on a warning. As VP of Product, Lee wasn't only responsible for adapting Artemis to meet the changing landscape. He was responsible for leading that adaptation, for showing others how to navigate the storm that was battering them.

But how fluent was he in the language of change himself?

Lee had always prided himself on his technical expertise, his problem-solving skills, but leading others through transformation required a different kind of fluency, a skill set he wasn't sure he possessed.

His father had adapted by starting over, but Lee had two hundred people counting on him to find a different way. Now, facing both Delta's disruption and his team's uncertainty, he felt like a tourist with a phrase book trying to navigate a foreign country.

The Call

Lee's neural display pinged with an incoming call notification, the CEO's name flashing with an urgent priority marker. His stomach tightened as he accepted.

Our success is determined by our ability to **become fluent with *any* change.**

"Kwan." Elena's voice was razor-sharp, her holographic projection materializing in the robotaxi's confined space. The founder and CEO of Artemis rarely made direct calls, especially this early. Her normally composed features were tight with barely contained fury.

"Have you seen the numbers?" Elena didn't wait for a response. "Delta has eaten our lunch."

"Elena, I—"

"Save it." Her avatar glanced at something off-screen. "Our board is in panic mode. I've authorized emergency measures across all divisions," Elena said, her voice dropping to a dangerous calm. "But Product is where we'll live or die in this fight. You need to find a solution, and fast."

Lee nodded slowly, his mind frozen.

"Talk to Ava. She's been mapping competitive disruption patterns for months. As our new head of Innovation, she has the authority to allocate whatever resources you need." Elena's gaze hardened. "But understand this, Lee. Your future at Artemis depends on how you handle the next few weeks. I'll let Ava decide your fate."

Before Lee could respond, Elena's projection dissolved, leaving him alone with the weight of her words. He'd heard rumors about Ava Loon: brilliant, unconventional, sometimes brutally direct. And now, she held his career in her hands.

The robotaxi continued its smooth journey toward Artemis campus, but Lee barely noticed, his mind fixed on a single thought: He needed to find Ava, immediately.

Arrival at the Artemis Campus

The robotaxi turned smoothly into the Artemis campus, its navigation system highlighting the famous Gardens in soft blue light through the smart glass. Like everything else in South Lake Union, the campus was a testament to the tech industry's transformation of Seattle—from industrial wasteland to innovation hub in a single generation. "We have arrived at your destination," the AI announced, as another message flashed across Lee's phone: "Go talk to Ava in the Gardens. She's expecting you."

"Thanks for topping up your trip with carbon offset credits. Have an amazing day!" the robotaxi added cheerfully, its doors whisking open to the perpetually misty Seattle morning.

Carbon-neutral—that's more efficient than our last product sprint, Lee thought, rolling his eyes.

He stepped out, facing the gleaming letters of Artemis mounted on the building, each one a promise he'd made to his team, his daughter, and his father's memory. His division led Artemis' AI initiatives, but while they'd been carefully building guardrails and safety protocols, Delta had been building the future.

He typed back quickly to Teresa: "Wouldn't miss it. But first, I need to have a conversation that might change everything."

Looking up at Artemis' towering headquarters, Lee felt the weight of three generations pressing in: his father's unfulfilled dreams, his own tenuous success, and his daughter's boundless faith in a future that was slipping away by the second. The old Lee would have retreated into defensive posturing, protecting what they'd built. But standing there, watching the morning sun break through Seattle's eternal clouds, he realized that saving Artemis would require something else entirely—the courage to burn down what they'd built so something new could rise from the ashes.

He took a deep breath of cool Pacific air. *This is going to be one long week.*

Somewhere in the Gardens, Ava was waiting to show him just how long it would be.

2
When Did Cowboys Go Extinct?

Casual in Converse

As Lee walked toward the Artemis gardens to meet Ava, he found his mind wandering back to the first time he'd seen Ava, head of Innovation.

It was the fall town hall at Artemis; the energy in the room was palpable with anticipation. There Ava was, standing at the front, exuding a warm and gentle acknowledgment that invited the team members in, creating an immediate sense of inclusion.

She stood out from the rest of the executive team in her simple black T-shirt, dark blue jeans, and a pair of classic Converse sneakers.

It's curious that she didn't suit up with everybody else, Lee thought. It didn't seem like Ava felt as if she was better than anyone else in the room. *She doesn't seem to be carrying an ego. Relatable, in fact. Not at all what I expected from someone the CEO entrusted with saving the company.*

She began to address the team: "With summer winding down, I'm glad I took the time for rest and relaxation." Ava laughed. "It's about to get hotter in the fall as our competition heats up."

She gently touched her heart for a split second. "I'm Ava. As some of you may know, I'm proud to originally be from Vancouver, just over the border from here—particularly having grown up on the traditional territories of the Squamish, Tsleil-Waututh, and Musqueam Nations. As I've dug deeper into my personal reconciliation plan, one thing that I appreciate the most about the Squamish is the Seventh Generation Principle that they bring to life in their discussions and decision-making.

"The Seventh Generation Principle, part of Indigenous philosophy, is to make decisions today that will result in a sustainable world seven generations down the road. At a minimum, that feels like 150 years from now. Just last week, I ran through Discovery Park and couldn't help but notice how beautiful the forest was, how well these trails have been maintained. The Indigenous Nations clearly bring that principle to life.

"I wonder how we might incorporate some of their wisdom into our own teachings..." Ava trailed off, mid-thought. She was clearly ruminating on her own question in real time.

It felt like she meant it. This wasn't the same mere virtue-signaling land acknowledgment that Lee had seen a million times over. He found himself slowly nodding along with Ava. Then, she turned the conversation in a whole new direction.

"Does anybody know when cowboys went extinct?"

When Cowboys Went Extinct

The team members in the room turned to one another quizzically.

"Throughout the early 1900s," said Ava, "every little boy and girl wanted to be a cowboy or cowgirl when they grew up. Think of the films of that era, the gun-slinging Westerns where the livelihood of the entire town was at stake with sheriffs fighting off robbers—and cowboys came to the rescue. The toys that flew off the shelves were all variations of cowboys, leather hats, boots, and pistols. There was a period of time when cowboys were *the* thing. Cowboys were in demand."

"So, when did cowboys go extinct?" Ava repeated the question gently, then offered a few answers.

"Was it when the first gas-powered automobile came along, in 1886 with Carl Benz, whose company is now Mercedes-Benz—or the first mass-produced automobiles, in 1903 with the Oldsmobile?

"Maybe the defining moment was when the world witnessed the Wright brothers fly up and down the Hudson River in 1909."

Ava paused. "Perhaps cowboys went extinct when the astronauts landed on the moon in 1969.

"You see, as soon as Neil Armstrong and the team landed on the moon, astronauts became the craze. Toy stores filled with action figures and paraphernalia, and the Wild, Wild West was quickly forgotten. Nobody cared about cowboys anymore."

"In fact," Ava added as an afterthought, "this very idea became the beautiful foundation for my favorite Disney-Pixar movie, *Toy Story*. Andy discards Woody, the cowboy, his once favored possession, for Buzz Lightyear, the Space Ranger!

Change doesn't just happen to us; **it happens through us.**

"This pattern reveals something crucial about Change Fluency," Ava continued, her eyes scanning the room to ensure her message was landing.

"With the drift winds of innovation, innovation gets created first, and ecosystems of adoption trail behind. Innovation sparks; adoption lags. Cowboys didn't disappear the moment cars were invented; it took years for the ecosystem and culture to fully transform.

"Those who develop fluency in adaptation see the signals earlier. They recognize that disruption isn't just happening to them, it's an invitation to evolve. Remember, change doesn't just happen *to* us; it happens *through* us too."

Lee found himself nodding. The concept of Change Fluency resonated, not just responding to disruption after it arrives but developing the capacity to anticipate and flow with it.

Ava clearly possessed this fluency, while his team still struggled with the basics; they hit their limit ordering beer in Spanish at an all-inclusive resort.

Her curly hair seemed to mirror the dynamic energy she brought into the room while her sharp hazel eyes sparkled with intelligence and a hint of wonder, as if she was on the verge of having a new idea.

Despite her casual attire, Ava had an undeniable aura of authority as she transitioned to addressing the rapid pace of a new competitor, Delta Tech.

Threat on the Horizon

"Look. I hear the rumors about Delta Tech, which has rave reviews about being super intuitive. Their models are complex. Their product features feel frictionless."

Despite what she was saying, Lee noted how Ava's calm demeanor underscored her confidence in their ability to not just keep up but to lead in the market.

"It's okay that Delta is leading the charge now. This allows us to check if our product road map is matching the market. But we see them. I believe that we're all still playing in the Wild West. And yes, that includes Delta. Space has not yet been discovered.

"So, how do we evolve from cowboys to astronauts? Buzz-fucking-Lightyear level innovation?" As Ava swore nonchalantly, an exec visibly tensed up. *Was she allowed to say that?*

With conviction, Ava outlined a clear path forward, filled with opportunities for innovation.

"Remember," Ava emphasized, "to disrupt is to differentiate, not be derivative. We're not looking to copy product features here; we're on a mission to reshape how work gets done. Imagine a world where AI agents have elevated our knowledge work, so we spend most of our time exercising our creativity instead of proving our administrative ability."

The room stirred. These words ignited a sense of purpose in Lee. *It would be awesome to get to work with her more closely. She seems like she's on the cusp of something transformative.*

Lee could see in that moment that Ava wasn't just a leader; she was a catalyst for change. He felt a growing excitement about the journey ahead.

Lee stopped in his tracks as he snapped back to the present. He had reached his destination: the Gardens. An open collaborative space where teams frequently connected.

He scanned the room and quickly found Ava, who was leaning against the coffee bar chatting with another colleague. She was wearing similar clothes to what she had on when Lee had first seen her at the Artemis town hall.

No shit. Maybe she's one of those minimalist tech execs who wears the same outfit every day to reduce decisions in her life, Lee thought, laughing to himself.

His levity quickly faded as Elena's words echoed in his mind: "I'll let Ava decide your fate."

The morning sun filtered through the Gardens' glass panels, casting long shadows across the collaborative space. Delta's numbers still burned in his mind—three hundred million users in a week! The weight of that reality pressed against his chest as he watched Ava wrap up her conversation. In that moment, he realized this wouldn't just be another strategy meeting. This was his DEFCON 1 moment, his chance to either transform Artemis or watch his career fade into irrelevance.

Time to go see what's up.

Key Takeaways & Considerations

Disruption isn't only about technology; it's about fundamental shifts in how value is created and perceived. Just as cowboys didn't disappear overnight, industries don't become obsolete in an instant. The transformation happens gradually, then suddenly.

Leadership Insights

1 **Change Requires Context:** Historical patterns help us understand present disruptions. The best leaders help teams see beyond immediate threats to broader patterns. Context creates clarity around the necessity for change.

2 **Authenticity in Transformation:** Effective change leaders demonstrate genuine care about impact (e.g., Ava's land acknowledgment), a willingness to address difficult truths directly, and the ability to make complex concepts relatable.

3 **Story as Strategy:** Metaphors and narratives help teams process complex change, understand market dynamics, and see beyond immediate challenges by connecting present struggles to historical patterns.

Warning Signs of Impending Disruption

- Established patterns become less relevant.
- New technologies reshape user expectations.
- Traditional roles are redefined.
- Market leadership is based on legacy rather than innovation.

Put It into Practice: Disruption Readiness Compass

How ready are you to wrestle with disruption? To help you apply your learnings throughout this book, we have built an AI Coach (Jay AI) that is trained on the Change Fluency methodology, as well as downloadable exercises and workbooks for you to fill in.

Simply scan the QR code or head on over to changefluency.com/bookresources to take action. For this chapter, look for the **Disruption Readiness Compass**.

3
Dancing with Disruption

The Season of Sleepless Nights

The Gardens combined the best of modern architecture with nature, a living metaphor for the intersection of innovation and organic growth that Artemis had always championed. As Lee waited for Ava to finish her conversation, he couldn't help but notice how the sharp wooden structures worked as aesthetic accents against the flush perimeter of flowers and trees, creating a space that somehow felt both engineered and alive.

"Ava?" Lee ventured, immediately regretting how tentative his voice sounded. "Elena mentioned you wanted to see me?"

Ava's warm smile cut through his anxiety. "Lee! Yes! Thanks for joining me on such short notice." She didn't waste any time with pleasantries. "Tell me, what do you believe our relationship with disruption is?"

The philosophical nature of the question caught Lee off guard. During the taxi ride, he'd mentally prepared to discuss market analysis, competitor breakdowns, and action plans—anything to convince her he was worth keeping around after Elena's ultimatum. But not this.

"You know," Ava said, studying his expression, "I heard about Elena's call this morning."

Lee stiffened. "Look, I understand the stakes—"

"Relax," Ava interrupted, a mischievous glint in her eye. "I'm not planning your exit interview just yet. Elena gets . . . dramatic when she's anxious. Don't worry about her 'deciding your fate' comment. You won't be fired." She paused, then added with mock seriousness, "Maybe."

Despite himself, Lee laughed, some of the tension draining from his shoulders.

"The truth is," Ava continued, "we're all facing disruption right now: the company, our teams, our competitors. What matters isn't Elena's panic or Delta's numbers but how we respond."

"I . . ." he started, then stopped. Through the Gardens' glass panels, he could see a robotaxi gliding silently past, its smooth movement a stark contrast to the chaos he felt internally. "I suppose right now our relationship with disruption is one of fear."

Ava gently nodded her head, her eyes twinkling with a familiar mix of intelligence and empathy.

"I remember when my partner and I had our first child," she began, gesturing for him to join her to sit in the Gardens' ergonomic chairs.

Lee checked his neural display again. Delta's numbers weren't going away. "With all due respect, Ava, I'm not sure how your parenting experience helps us with Delta stealing three hundred million of our users."

Ava's eyes flickered with something . . . Annoyance? Challenge? But then, she laughed. "Humor me for two minutes. I promise there's a point."

We can't drive innovation without **first championing change.**

The Gardens' smart lighting adjusted as they sat, creating a more intimate atmosphere. Lee found himself reluctantly settling in, his fingers still itching to check the user migration data.

"We were so anxious. We knew that our lives would be disrupted—in theory—but had no idea how it would play out in reality. We went to all the prenatal classes, read all the books on how to take care of a baby, and spoke to all our friends who were parents. But nothing could quite prepare us for what was to come. Then, our daughter, Hailey, was born. And what an absolute shit show that was."

The profanity made Lee laugh despite himself, and he thought of his own children, Grace and Audrey.

"You see," Ava continued, "I used to get so much sleep—ten hours each night. But then when Hailey came along, we were thrown into these three-hour sprints of feeding, burping, changing. For the first six months, I barely slept. And when I don't get sleep, I'm literally the worst person in the world; I wouldn't want my worst enemy to spend time with me!

"And it's not just the disruption itself that overwhelms us," Ava continued, her gaze shifting outside, where Seattle's tech corridor buzzed with activity. "It's the pace."

She pulled up a visualization in the air between them. "The speed of change is increasing. The amount of information we have is doubling every seventy-two hours. We take seventeen photos of the same moment. Only one is needed, the rest archived.

"We're confronting an exponential acceleration of change, and our brains simply aren't wired for it. That's why our initial response is almost always resistance."

The Gardens' embedded screens, which had been listening to their conversation, flickered with images of people scrolling endless social feeds, backing up photos that would never be seen again, saving articles never to be read.

"It's like trying to drink from a fire hose," Lee observed.

"Exactly. And that's why our relationship with disruption needs to evolve. Not just to accept change but to develop new ways of processing and prioritizing it."

Resistant to Disruption

"As I think about my relationship with disruption," Ava continued, her gaze steady, "it's usually one of resistance. After all, I'm happy with my current state. I really like my ways of working and operating!"

"Getting hit by disruption throws us off balance," she said, leaning forward. "It pushes us to push back with a tremendous amount of resistance. Simultaneously, designing a new normal requires significant effort. Navigating the new norm requires intentionality."

Lee thought about Artemis' own transformation attempts over the years. The failed initiatives, the resistance to change, the comfort with their success that had perhaps left them vulnerable to Delta's disruption.

"And we all know the stats," Ava continued. "Seventy percent of those transformations fail. But rather than being thrown off course, or even blown away, by disruption, how do we find agency in driving change and innovation in our organizations?"

The question hung in the air between them, a challenge and an invitation wrapped into one. Lee found himself thinking of his daughter Grace's science fair project, that crude but earnest neural network designed to recognize dog breeds. "It only gets it right about 60 percent of the time right now," Grace had said. "But that's okay because even AIs have to learn and grow."

Maybe that was the point. Maybe the relationship with disruption wasn't about getting it right all the time but about learning to grow through the uncertainty.

"I'm not concerned with Delta's technology," Ava said, as if reading his thoughts. "We all know that what they launched is better than what we have. What I *am* concerned with is our culture." She stood up, walking toward one of the Gardens' embedded screens to highlight a specific area. "Specifically, our comfort with the status quo."

The words hit Lee like a physical force. He thought about all the times in recent years when his team had chosen the safer path, the known outcome, the incremental improvement over the revolutionary change. How many times had he himself said, "That's not how we do things here" or "Let's stick to what we know works"?

"You know what I've noticed, Lee?" Ava continued, her voice gentle but probing. "When I walk through our development floors, I see some of the brightest minds in tech. But I also see something else—I see people who've gotten too comfortable with being the market leader. They're like new parents who've finally gotten their baby to sleep through the night: so afraid of disrupting that peace that they tiptoe around, avoiding any change that might upset the balance."

Lee felt a flush of recognition. Hadn't he just been longing for the comfort of Artemis' former market position? The safety of being the undisputed leader in their space?

She turned to face him fully. "You see it, too, don't you? The way our engineers lovingly maintain code bases that should have been retired years ago? How our product managers tweak existing features instead of imagining entirely new paradigms? The way our leaders"—she paused meaningfully—"celebrate stability over innovation?"

"Yet what's fascinating about disruption is that it is a lot like language acquisition," Ava added, leaning forward with newfound energy. "When we first encounter a new language, everything feels overwhelming. We struggle with pronunciation, grammar rules, cultural contexts. But with repeated exposure, we develop something linguists call 'muscle memory'—neural pathways that transform conscious effort into fluid expression."

She gestured to the Gardens' ambient systems. "Change Fluency works the same way. The first major disruption feels catastrophic. The second, challenging but manageable. By the fifth or sixth, you're not just surviving; you're translating disruption into opportunity almost instinctively."

"So, you're saying we need practice being disrupted?" Lee asked skeptically.

"I'm saying disruption is inevitable. The question isn't whether it will come, but whether we'll use each experience to develop deeper fluency." Ava smiled. "You see, contrary to popular opinion, disruption is healthy. It's natural. It forces us to rethink how everything works. This whole Delta thing feels like an opportunity for us to break patterns—to innovate. But we can't drive innovation without first championing change."

Lee took Ava's last comment into serious consideration. He'd faced technological shifts before, but had he truly learned from each one or merely survived them? Had he developed fluency or just memorized a few emergency phrases?

Lee nodded slowly, thinking of his own resistance to radical changes in their development process. "We've become like overprotective parents," he realized aloud. "So

How we interpret and respond to change determines whether **we're managing change— or creating it.**

focused on preserving what we have that we're not letting our child—I mean, our organization—grow and evolve."

"Exactly." Ava's eyes lit up. "And that's just one of the chains holding us back. You see, there are five chains of change. Five fundamental barriers that keep organizations trapped in their comfort zones, unable to embrace transformation. Our comfort with the status quo? That's just the beginning."

She turned to the screen, speaking to its AI interface. "Aria, pull up the Change Fluency playbook." As the display came to life, Lee felt something shift inside him—a readiness to confront not only Delta's disruption but also the comfortable patterns that had made that disruption possible in the first place.

Lee realized that his relationship with disruption was about to be transformed—just like those sleepless nights with a newborn had transformed Ava's relationship with disruption. The question wasn't whether disruption would come but how they would choose to meet it.

Later, as Lee and Ava exited the Gardens, they passed a group of consultants huddled around a digital whiteboard. "We need to leverage our synergies to disrupt the paradigm with a scalable, robust solution that drives actionable insights through our digital transformation journey," one said with complete seriousness, while the others nodded vigorously and took notes.

Lee caught Ava's eye, and they both stifled laughter as they rounded the corner. "I think he just won buzzword bingo," Ava whispered, "and possibly invented a new language only understood by our AI."

Key Takeaways & Considerations

Our Initial Response to Disruption Is Natural but Not Final

Change triggers an instinctive resistance in most organizations, much like our bodies reacting to stress. However, this initial response can evolve into intentional adaptation when we understand that disruption is inevitable. The goal isn't to eliminate our reaction to change but to develop our capacity to move through it more effectively.

Navigation Requires Understanding Our Current Patterns

How we respond to disruption today shapes how we'll handle future transformations. Organizations that thrive don't just survive change; they study their responses to it, learning from both successes and setbacks. By understanding our patterns, we can begin to shift from reactive resistance to proactive adaptation.

Transformation Happens at the Speed of Awareness

The average organization undergoes three major transformations every five years, but success isn't determined by the frequency of disruption—it's shaped by our relationship with it. When we move from fighting change to understanding it, we create space for both concerns and possibilities, allowing transformation to unfold more naturally.

What's Your Change Mindset?

Ever wonder why some people thrive during disruption while others seem to crumble under pressure? Our research at the Change Fluency Co. reveals that how we navigate change comes down to two key factors:

1   How we interpret change (threat vs. opportunity)
2   How we respond to it (resistant vs. adaptive)

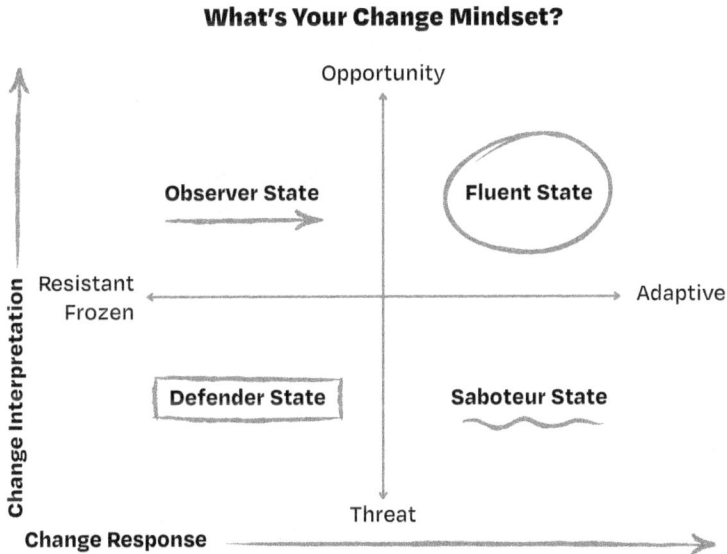

What's Your Change Mindset?

Opportunity

Observer State

Fluent State

Resistant
Frozen

Adaptive

Change Interpretation

Defender State

Saboteur State

Threat

Change Response

The Change Mindset Matrix

There are four distinct change mindsets:

Defender State (Threat-Focused + Resistant)

"We've been doing it this way for years. I built this myself."

Defenders see transformation as an attack on established systems. They grasp tightly to what they know, repeatedly saying, "This is how I've always done it" while overanalyzing risks to avoid change. They focus intensely on what they might lose rather than what they could gain. They keep up their defensive behaviors until forced to change by circumstances beyond their control.

Observer State (Opportunity-Focused + Resistant)

"I'll wait to see what happens. There are definitely some possibilities here."

Observers intellectually recognize opportunities but remain stuck in their regular ways of working. They constantly compare themselves to peers and become paralyzed when facing uncertainty, oscillating between frantic analysis and complete inaction. They wait for perfect clarity before acting.

Saboteur State (Threat-Focused + Adaptive)

"I'll smile and say I support this, but..."

These individuals appear supportive of change on the surface but actively undermine efforts. They're adaptive in their resistance—finding creative ways to derail initiatives and maintaining plausible deniability through passive-aggressive compliance and strategic delays.

Fluent State (Opportunity-Focused + Adaptive)
"Change happens through us. I'd love to be part of this."

These are your change champions who assume every disruption contains opportunity. When balanced with thoughtful consideration, their excitement becomes a powerful catalyst for meaningful transformation. They recognize resistance as information rather than opposition, creating space for both enthusiasm and concern while moving forward thoughtfully.

The Strategic Distinction: To vs. Through

The critical insight: Those on the left side of the matrix believe change happens *to* us; we're victims of circumstances. Those sitting on the right side of the matrix believe that change happens *through* us—we're change fluent (for better or worse). How we interpret and respond to change determines whether we're managing change—or creating it.

Put It into Practice: Our Typical Responses

Just as Ava's story about becoming a parent illustrated how our relationship with disruption evolves, how do you view your organization's current response patterns to change?

Simply scan the QR code or head on over to changefluency.com/bookresources to take action. For this chapter, look for **Our Typical Responses**.

4
Customer Exodus

Real-Time Impact

Lee's augmented-reality display flickered with urgent notifications as he scanned through the morning's metrics. His team's daily standup was starting in two minutes, but the latest numbers from Delta demanded his attention. He gestured through the holographic charts, each swipe revealing another concerning trend.

"Product engagement down 12 percent since Delta's launch," his AI assistant noted. "User session length decreased by 23 percent."

"Show me feature adoption rates," Lee commanded, his stomach tightening. The visualization shifted, revealing a stark comparison between Artemis' collaboration tools and Delta's new offerings.

Jess Bang, his lead Product Manager, materialized in his AR field of view. Like all remote participants, her avatar was nearly indistinguishable from physical presence, though the slight blue glow marked her as joining from Seattle's east side.

"Lee, we're losing key enterprise accounts." Jess's voice was tense. "Quantum Computing Inc. just announced they're migrating their entire workforce to Delta's platform by end of quarter. That's twenty thousand seats."

"Pull up the migration data," Lee requested. A new visualization appeared, showing a real-time feed of enterprise customer activity. Red dots pulsed across the globe, each representing a company evaluating or actively planning migration to Delta's platform.

"It's not just the AI capabilities," Jess continued. "Their integration layer is making our ecosystem look... obsolete. Teams are building workflows we never imagined."

Lee nodded as he studied the pattern of customer migrations. After six years leading product teams at Artemis, he'd learned to read between the lines of data. This wasn't just feature adoption or user preferences; this was an existential threat to their entire platform strategy.

"Schedule an emergency product council for this afternoon," he decided. "And Jess? Let's have the team prepare migration prevention scenarios. I want options on my desk before the executive meeting."

Executive Tensions

The storm outside matched Lee's mood as he entered the executive conference room. Seattle's perpetual drizzle had transformed into sheets of rain that battered against the floor-to-ceiling windows, turning the Space Needle into a ghostly silhouette in the distance. Inside, the tension was equally palpable.

Lee had called this emergency meeting of Artemis' senior leadership team, something he wouldn't have dared do even a week ago. But Delta's numbers had changed everything. Three hundred million users in a week wasn't just disruption—it felt like a flare gun that had gone off, signaling that they might all have to start looking for jobs if they didn't address this head-on. And soon. Like, now.

Maya Chen, VP of Operations, caught Lee's eye as he entered. Her presence was both a comfort and a concern; they'd worked together before she'd taken a role at Google, and her return to Artemis had been seen as a major win for their operations team. But as sharp as Maya was, she was quick to bulldoze ideas that didn't meet the needs of Operations.

"Before we begin," Lee started, his voice steadier than he felt, "I want to thank everyone for making time on such short notice." He glanced around the room: Charles Morton from Finance, his perpetual scowl deeper than usual; Sarah Williams from Development, already shaking her head at whatever she anticipated coming; Marcus Chan from Marketing, furiously typing on his neural interface.

"We all know what matters now," Lee continued, bringing up the morning's metrics. "Delta's three hundred million users in a week. Their AI capabilities that make ours look outdated. Their market momentum that's threatening everything we've built." The numbers hung in the air between them, stark and challenging.

"A moment of panic, you mean," Charles interrupted, his British accent sharp. "We've run the numbers, Lee. To match Delta's capabilities, we'd need to double our AI research budget at minimum."

Sarah piled on: "Which feels impossible for Development to do as I lose engineer after engineer to Delta. Especially in this market—"

"Actually," a familiar voice cut through the tension, "we're focusing on the wrong problem entirely."

Lee turned to see Ava entering the room, carrying that peculiar mix of authority and approachability that had first caught Lee's attention at the town hall.

"Ava." Maya straightened in her chair. "I didn't realize you'd be joining us."

Before Ava could respond, Maya pulled up a diagram on a piece of paper. Unlike the other executives with their holographic displays, Maya had sketched her infrastructure diagrams by hand—a habit from her Google days when she'd discovered thinking slowed down just enough with pen and paper to catch critical details others missed.

"But since you're here, look at our infrastructure strain. Every time users switch to Delta, our systems have to maintain backward compatibility while operating at reduced capacity. We're burning twice the computing resources to serve half the users.

"It's like watching someone try to bail out the *Titanic* with a teaspoon while the band plays a corporate strategy remix. Sure, the music sounds nice, but we're still sinking."

Lee studied the cascade of alerts flooding his neural display: customer migrations, TechMinds' resignation threats, and now Maya's infrastructure warnings. TechMinds was a recently acquired company that had joined the Artemis team; seeing people threaten to leave so quickly was concerning. Each problem demanded immediate attention, yet addressing any single one would mean neglecting the others.

Maya's hands moved with military precision as she manipulated the data. Her time in Big Tech had honed her operational instincts; she could smell a system collapse before the first warning lights appeared.

"This feels like the classic case of *death by a thousand cuts*," Lee said, the realization hitting him. "We have so

When everything is urgent, **nothing gets done well.**

many competing priorities that every proposed action becomes painful. Our teams are either burning out trying to tackle everything or becoming resistant because they're unsure which direction will actually stick a year from now."

Ava nodded, her casual demeanor shifting to something more focused. "That's exactly what the first chain of change looks like in action: *Clutter and Chaos.* When everything is urgent, nothing gets done well. We're not just losing market share; we're losing our ability to respond effectively because we're scattered across too many fronts.

"Lee asked me to share some insights about transformation," Ava continued, smiling as she moved to the front of the room. "But first, let's talk about the question everyone's asking: What matters now? Delta's numbers. Their technology. Their momentum." She paused, letting the words settle. "It's a natural question, but it's the wrong one."

She gestured to the room's AI interface. "Aria, display the Change Fluency framework."

The room's ambient lighting dimmed as a holographic diagram materialized in the center of the conference table. Five interconnected chains floated in the air, each one labeled and slowly rotating.

The Five Chains of Change

"These are the five chains of change," Ava explained, her voice carrying across the hushed room. "Five fundamental barriers that prevent organizations from developing true Change Fluency—and ultimately leaving them unable to embrace transformation.

"First, we have Clutter and Chaos. This is an organizational-level chain that manifests when teams face multiple mandates and constantly changing directions. Everything happens so quickly that individuals fail to prioritize effectively."

The first chain pulsed with a soft blue light as she continued.

"Second, Comfort with the Status Quo. This chain operates at the individual level. People become so comfortable with existing processes that they struggle to find motivation for change. It's particularly strong when people have personal attachments to current systems they've built."

She moved to the third chain. "Competing Interests, measured at both organizational and team levels. Despite rolling up to a corporate scorecard, different departments often have conflicting metrics and goals."

The fourth chain brightened. "Constraints: financial resources, time, talent, competency. While most leaders point to insufficient resources as the reason for transformation failure, high-performing organizations learn to work within their constraints better."

"And finally"—Ava touched the last chain, making it glow a deep indigo—"Apathy. This individual-level chain manifests as disengagement, often due to burnout, change fatigue, or frustration with constantly shifting priorities."

The Five Chains of Change

1 Clutter and Chaos
2 Comfort with the Status Quo
3 Competing Interests
4 Constraints
5 Apathy

The holographic chains rotated slowly above the conference table as Ava concluded her introduction. Charles was the first to break the silence.

Bloody Bleeding

"Fascinating framework," he said, British accent sharp with sarcasm, "but it doesn't address our immediate reality. We're bloody bleeding market share. My team's projections show a 40 percent revenue decline if we don't match Delta's capabilities this quarter."

"Did you just say 'bloody bleeding'? Isn't that redundant?" Maya laughed.

"You know what I mean." Charles glared at her. "We're not just losing market share; we're hemorrhaging it faster than a start-up's seed funding."

"What if we're looking at this all wrong?" Lee found himself speaking up, surprising even himself. The morning's data visualization was still fresh in his mind. "The chains Ava's showing us—especially this first one about Clutter and Chaos—it's not just about our organization. It's about our product strategy."

Sarah nodded vigorously, then quipped, "Our latest user research shows overwhelming feature fatigue. Teams are using less than 20 percent of our platform's capabilities."

"So, you're suggesting we strip down our platform?" Charles looked incredulous. "That's suicide."

"No." Lee stood, using his neural interface to pull up the morning's migration data. "I'm suggesting we break free of our own chains. We're not losing because we lack features. We're losing because we've created so much complexity that we've lost sight of what matters most to our users."

Maya leaned forward. "Lee's right. At Google, I watched teams chase feature parity until they lost their soul. Maybe our first challenge isn't Delta. It's our own chaos."

"Exactly." Ava smiled, making the first chain glow brighter than the others. "Before we can challenge Delta, we need to master our own chaos. I've dropped an article on Nintendo in our exec channel—read it by tomorrow morning. They faced a similar moment of truth, and their response might surprise you."

The rain had softened to a gentle patter against the windows, its rhythm matching the slow rotation of the holographic chains. As the executives filed out, Lee lingered, watching the chains fade from view. Something fundamental had shifted today. They hadn't just named their chains; they'd identified the first one they needed to break. As Ava had said, before they could challenge Delta, they needed to master their own chaos.

Reflections in the Glass

The evening light filtered through the Gardens' smart glass, automatically adjusting to reduce glare. Lee stood with Ava by the digital whiteboard, where their earlier holographic presentation had left ghostly traces in the display's memory.

"You surprised yourself in there," Ava observed, studying Lee's expression.

"I surprised everyone," Lee admitted. "Six months ago, I would have been the first one pushing to match Delta feature for feature. But seeing those migration patterns this morning..." He gestured, pulling up a simplified version of the visualization. "We've been so focused on what we *could* build, we lost sight of what we *should* build."

"And now?"

"Now I need to convince my team to embrace constraint as a feature, not a bug. We've got senior engineers who've spent years building systems they're proud of. Telling them we need to simplify, to potentially discard their work..." He trailed off.

"That's why understanding these chains matters," Ava noted. "Change isn't just about the direction—it's about the resistance we'll face getting there."

Lee nodded, already mentally planning how to approach his team. Breaking their chains of change would require more than just a new product strategy. It would demand a fundamental shift in how they approached innovation itself.

He gazed across a skyline dotted with AR advertisements for Delta's platform, a constant reminder of the challenge ahead. But for the first time since the crisis began, Lee felt something close to clarity.

Through the clearing sky, the Space Needle stood sharp against the horizon, a reminder that sometimes you had to rise above the immediate to see the essential.

Key Takeaways & Considerations

Clutter and Chaos

Clutter and Chaos is a chain of change that should largely be measured at the *organizational* level. The organization fails to move forward due to clutter across teams.

With multiple mandates and leadership constantly changing direction, teams feel the pull and strain of many fast-paced directives. The culture begins to feel like initiatives start up quickly, then come to a breakneck stop.

Everything is happening so quickly that individuals fail to prioritize.

Comfort with the Status Quo

Comfort with the Status Quo is measured at the *individual* level. Individuals are so comfortable that they struggle to find a desire to grow. After all, if things aren't broken, why try to fix them?

This chain isn't just about comfort though; it's also about ownership. Because people own specific responsibilities, budgets, and portfolios, they have a personal attachment to the current state. They may have built the operating manuals or walk-through guides or established an entirely new department five years ago—asking them to give that up for something else is extremely difficult.

Competing Interests

Competing Interests is measured at the *organizational* and *team* levels. It is customary and anticipated that most organizational groups and departments receive new metrics on their KPI scorecard annually to target. And yet despite rolling up to a corporate scorecard, functional departments tend to have metrics unique to their group.

For example, Sales has to grow 25 percent year over year, Operations has to cut 12 percent in its operating budget and delivery time, Dev and Engineering has to deliver four new product lines that were on the backlog (and not on Sales' wish list), which require an expansion of Operations' operating budget, and Marketing has to reach twenty million impressions and mentions across the social media universe (which, of course, will likely require more spend than last year).

The mere fact that competing interests exist across most organizations continues to fuel the demand for thought leadership and guidance around collaboration and teamwork. Some companies might not *even have* scorecards and KPIs—so they won't even realize that they have competing interests!

Constraints

Constraints is a chain of change measured at the *organizational* level. There may be multiple constraints that form an organizational sandbox, such as financial resources, time, talent, and competency.

When a transformation fails, most leaders immediately point to the fact that insufficient and inappropriate levels of resources were allocated to operating budgets, training, or capacity.

Most people think that throwing more resources at the problem is the solution, when the truth is that high-performing organizations teach teams how to work within their constraints better.

Apathy

A key factor holding back change initiatives is Apathy. This chain of change is measured at the *individual* level.

Individuals check out for a multitude of reasons, such as burnout, change fatigue, frustration with constantly changing imperatives, being overlooked for promotions, corporate politics, and more.

This, of course, leads to disengagement. Over the past few years, about 77 percent of employees have been disengaged, costing organizations an estimated $7.8 trillion annually (11 percent of global GDP).

Each of these five chains represents not just an obstacle to change but a specific barrier to developing Change Fluency.

By understanding which chains most constrain your organization, you can focus your transformation efforts on breaking free from these limitations and creating space for developing the adaptive capacity you need for innovation that sticks and stands out.

Put It into Practice: The Five Chains of Change

Understanding what's holding your organization back is the first step toward meaningful transformation. Like a climber surveying the mountain before choosing their path, you need to identify which chains of change are most constraining your progress.

Simply scan the QR code or head on over to changefluency.com/bookresources to take action. For this chapter, click on **The Five Chains of Change** to take the complimentary assessment.

5
Zoom Out
to Zoom In

Seventeen Useless Presentations and Counting

The predawn Gardens were silent except for the gentle
hum of data streams flowing through smart glass panels,
each one reflecting Lee's growing desperation.

News had broken overnight that Sarah Williams, Artemis' head of Development, had quit. What's worse? She
had gone over to Delta.

Lee had been there since 4 a.m., neural display cycling
through presentation scenarios for the emergency board
meeting. Each projection reinforced the same devastating
trend that Charles had mentioned at the executive meeting:
user migration patterns leading to a 40 percent revenue
decline if they couldn't match Delta's capabilities.

The news about Sarah certainly exacerbated things. And
despite Ava's encouragement, it would only reinforce Elena's
worst fears about Artemis' future—and possibly his own.

"Your cortisol levels suggest you haven't slept," Ava
noted, materializing beside him. She gestured at his neural
feeds. "How many versions of that presentation have you
made?"

"Seventeen," Lee admitted. "And none of them solve our real problem."

"Which is?"

"That's just it. I'm not even sure what our real problem is anymore." Lee ran his hands through his disheveled hair. "We've got the TechMinds integration imploding, Sarah's departure is already triggering an exodus, Delta's quantum breakthrough, customer migrations... Our teams are being pulled in every single direction..." He trailed off as the Gardens' smart glass flickered with another alert: three more enterprise customers announcing plans to switch platforms.

"Ah," Ava said with a nod, "it sounds like we're experiencing a common case of tyranny of the urgent."

"Tyranny of the *whatty*?"

"The *tyranny of the urgent*. It's when everything feels like a fire that needs to be put out immediately. Each crisis demands attention *now*, so we keep reacting instead of responding strategically. Like a firefighter running from blaze to blaze, never getting the chance to investigate what's starting all these fires in the first place."

Does Your Organization have a "Tyranny of the Urgent" Problem?

Does your team spend more time firefighting than forward planning? The tyranny of the urgent takes over when everything feels like an emergency—emails marked "ASAP," last-minute pivots, and constant crisis-mode decision-making. Instead of working strategically, leaders and teams are stuck reacting to immediate pressures, leaving no space to address root causes or drive long-term impact.

It's a cycle that leads to burnout, misalignment, and missed opportunities. If urgent requests always override long-term priorities, your organization may be trapped in survival mode rather than building for the future. That is a clear signal that you are struggling with the first chain of change, Clutter and Chaos. The next few chapters will unpack how to break free.

"That's exactly it," Lee said, gesturing at his neural feeds full of crisis alerts. "Every time I try to step back and think strategically, another urgent problem pulls me back in. It's like being trapped in a constant state of emergency."

"And that's our first chain of change: Clutter and Chaos," Ava replied. "When everything feels urgent, nothing feels clear."

She waved away his presentation projections and summoned a simple visualization in the air between them. Five interconnected chains rotated slowly, the first one pulsing with a soft blue light.

"Most organizations fail to move forward because they're paralyzed by multiple competing priorities and constant changes in direction. Everything happens so quickly that we lose the ability to distinguish between what's urgent and what's important. It's the classic tyranny of the urgent problem."

Lee stared at the rotating chain visualization, remembering how his father used to say that confusion was the first step toward clarity. "So, how do we break free from this chain?"

Change doesn't just happen to us; **it happens *through* us.**

Flustered as F**k

"Have you ever tried to drive a stick shift?" Ava asked unexpectedly, her question cutting through Lee's spiral of anxiety.

Lee blinked, momentarily thrown off. "What?"

"A manual transmission. My dad taught me when I was sixteen on this ancient Toyota Corolla," Ava continued, seemingly oblivious to Lee's confusion. "I stalled that car at least thirty times in the high school parking lot. Everyone watching, laughing. I was flustered as f**k."

Lee frowned, his eyebrows furrowing. "I'm failing to see how your teenage driving lessons relate to our extinction-level crisis with Delta."

"My dad said something I never forgot," Ava replied. "He told me, 'The best car anti-theft device is knowing how to drive stick shift.' Most thieves can't handle the complexity, so they move on to easier targets."

She gestured to the chaos of metrics hovering around them. "Look at Delta. They're moving at light speed, scaling faster than we can comprehend. Meanwhile, we're sitting here trying to understand how to respond, feeling overwhelmed and paralyzed."

"We're the stick shift in this analogy?" Lee asked skeptically.

"No." Ava smiled. "The crisis is the stick shift. And right now, you're stalling out because you're so focused on each individual pedal, each metric, each problem that you can't get the car moving. You're flustered because you're looking at the parts instead of the pattern."

Lee leaned back, considering. "So, how do I stop stalling?"

"The secret to driving stick isn't in mastering the clutch or the gas individually," Ava explained. "It's in understanding how they work together: seeing the pattern, feeling the rhythm. My dad made me close my eyes and just listen to the engine before trying again. When I stopped overthinking each individual movement and focused on the harmony of the whole system, suddenly I could drive."

Lee glanced at the Gardens' displays, seeing the scattered crisis metrics in a new light. "So, we need to stop fixating on each individual emergency..."

"... and start seeing the pattern they create together." Ava nodded. "That's exactly why we need to zoom out to zoom in. It's the first Innovation Principle, and it comes with a mindset shift." On the digital whiteboard, she wrote:

Mindset shift from clutter and chaos → clarity

Innovation Principle 1: Zoom Out to Zoom In

"Zoom out to zoom in," Ava repeated, dimming the Gardens' ambient lighting. "Let me tell you about another company that faced its own moment of overwhelming chaos. One that chose to look beyond the immediate noise to find the real signal."

"Zoom out to zoom in? That sounds like something my optometrist would say right before charging me for progressive lenses."

Ava laughed. "Hey, at least I'm not charging you for the irony—needing distance to see what's right in front of us. Though I do accept payment in coffee and existential realizations."

"Good thing the company cafeteria has an endless supply of both," Lee quipped, feeling a brief moment of lightness amid the crisis.

The holographic displays shifted, showing a simple image: a deck of playing cards from 1889 with a faded Nintendo logo on the back of them.

"Nintendo?" Lee's confusion had an edge of frustration. "We're facing an extinction-level crisis, and you want to talk about games?"

"I want to talk about seeing clearly when everything feels like chaos," Ava replied, her calm confidence suddenly making Lee want to shake her.

"While you give me a history lesson on *Donkey Kong*, Sarah is probably sharing our architecture with Delta's engineers!" Lee snapped, immediately regretting it.

Ava raised her eyebrows. "You know what? You're right. This is your division, your team. If you'd rather stick with what you've been doing—"

"No," Lee interrupted, surprising himself. "I'm sorry. I'm just..." He gestured helplessly at the crisis alerts flooding his neural display. "Keep going."

"In 1974, Hiroshi Yamauchi faced the same thing you're facing now: the terror of watching everything you've built become suddenly, devastatingly obsolete. His company had been making playing cards for eighty-five years. Their market was stable, their expertise unquestioned. Then, he visited a Magnavox manufacturing plant and saw the future of entertainment being built."

The Gardens' displays flickered with historical footage: assembly lines producing early video game consoles, workers testing primitive electronic displays, a world on the cusp of digital transformation.

"Yamauchi could have focused on the immediate chaos: new technology threatening their core business, competitors emerging from unexpected directions, skills gaps in his workforce. Instead, he did something remarkable." Ava paused, letting the significance build. "He watched how the workers interacted with the machines. But more importantly, he watched people's eyes light up when they first played the games."

Lee thought about his own cluttered neural feeds, each one demanding immediate attention. "He was looking for patterns in the noise," he said.

"Exactly. While others saw technical specifications and market threats, Yamauchi detected a deeper signal: the timeless human desire for play. He zoomed out to see beyond the immediate chaos."

The displays shifted to show Nintendo's journey through multiple disruptions: the video game crash of 1983, the transition to portable gaming, the rise of mobile devices. Each time, the company had faced overwhelming chaos. Each time, they'd found clarity by looking beyond surface-level trends.

"You're saying we need to be more like Mario—keep jumping even when the ground is falling away?" Lee asked.

Ava raised an eyebrow. "I was thinking more Zelda than Mario. Sometimes you need the wisdom to see what others miss, not just the courage to keep jumping."

"Great," Lee sighed. "Next you'll tell me I need to collect magical artifacts before the board meeting."

Ava opened her mouth to start to say something, but Lee noticed her eyes darting to an augmented alert on her display, "Oh shoot. My husband is calling me. I'll be right back, but if you haven't had the chance to read the Nintendo article, now is a great time."

She briskly walked off, picking up the call as she went. "Hey, babe, I'm just at work. What's up?"

Lee flicked his hand upward to the screen. "Aria, show Nintendo article."

From the Field
Nintendo's Lesson
in Perspective
Beyond the Game

The Paradox of Focus: Understanding Noise to Find Clarity

In 1985, the video game industry faced what seemed like terminal chaos. Revenue had plunged from $3.2 billion in 1983 to just $100 million in two years—a 97 percent collapse.

Most companies zoomed in on the immediate crisis—excess inventory, plummeting sales, retailer skepticism. But Nintendo's team, led by Yamauchi's son-in-law Minoru Arakawa, zoomed out to see broader patterns. They looked beyond the gaming industry and observed

- rising VCR sales (suggesting an appetite for home entertainment),

- strong board game sales (indicating a desire for family interaction), and

- peak TV viewing (showing demand for accessible entertainment).

It seemed that people weren't rejecting games; they were rejecting bad experiences.

This insight marked the first of several pivotal moments when Nintendo demonstrated the power of pattern recognition—seeing beyond surface-level market trends to identify deeper human needs and behaviors. Over the next three decades, the company would refine this ability into an art form, using it to revolutionize gaming in ways its competitors never imagined.

Nintendo's Three Moments of Clarity

Each of these moments illustrates a different aspect of how zooming out can reveal opportunities others miss. The first and perhaps most counterintuitive came with the development of what would become Nintendo's most successful portable device.

The Game Boy Revolution: Seeing Beyond Power

By 1989, Nintendo had proven it could revive a dead market. The Nintendo Entertainment System had transformed video games from a failed fad into a thriving industry, commanding 95 percent market share in home consoles. But now it faced a new challenge: portable gaming. Its competitors saw this as a technological arms race. Atari and Sega were pouring resources into creating miniature versions of home consoles, complete with color screens and advanced graphics. The industry consensus was clear: Whoever had the most impressive technical specifications would win the handheld war.

In this environment of technical one-upmanship, engineer Gunpei Yokoi made a curious observation during his train commute. Despite having magazines and newspapers available, businessmen were playing with pocket calculators to pass the time. They weren't playing with it because the calculator was entertaining; they were playing with it because it was accessible, portable, and had great battery life.

This observation led to the Game Boy's counterintuitive design that focused on

- battery life over graphics (Game Boy: 30+ hours, competitors: 3–5 hours),

- affordability over features (Game Boy: $89.99, competitors: $149.99+), and

- reliability over impressive specifications.

The market told the story: Atari's technically advanced Lynx sold just one million units. Sega's color-screened Game Gear reached 10.62 million. Meanwhile, Nintendo's "underpowered" Game Boy and its successors? An astounding 118.69 million units worldwide.

The Wii: Seeing Beyond Gamers

With the Game Boy's success, Nintendo had mastered the art of doing more with less. But by 2006, the gaming landscape had transformed dramatically. The PlayStation 2 had dominated the previous console generation, and now Sony and Microsoft were locked in an battle of processing power. Sony's PlayStation 3 boasted a revolutionary Cell processor that promised cinema-quality graphics. Microsoft's Xbox 360 advertised an advanced online gaming network and high-definition visuals. Market research showed hardcore gamers demanding more power, better graphics, and increasingly complex games.

Nintendo faced a critical decision. It could enter this expensive arms race, trying to compete on pure processing power—or it could find a different signal in the noise. Instead of following market research about what gamers wanted, Nintendo's research team conducted field studies with "extreme users": individuals who "hate playing games on gaming consoles." They identified usability challenges like controller complexity, which directly shaped the Wii's design. They found

- families wanting to play together but intimidated by complex controls,
- social gatherings breaking up when someone played games, and
- older adults interested in active entertainment.

These observations led to the Wii's revolutionary motion controls through the Wii Remote. It allowed players to interact with games through natural movements that mimicked swinging a tennis racket or steering a vehicle, resulting in a family-friendly design that resulted in

- 101.63 million units in sales,
- 45 percent female players (versus the industry average of 29 percent), and
- unprecedented adoption by older adults.

The Switch: Seeing Beyond Categories

By 2017, Nintendo had proven twice that understanding human behavior was more valuable than following industry trends. But now it faced perhaps its biggest challenge yet:

the complete fragmentation of gaming itself. The market had split into distinct, seemingly incompatible categories: consoles for serious gaming, smartphones for casual play, handhelds for gaming on the go. Each had its own user base, development approach, and business model. Market research showed these segments were distinct and should be treated as separate markets.

The conventional wisdom was clear: Choose a lane and excel in it. Instead, Nintendo's research team wondered if these rigid categories reflected how people actually wanted to play. Rather than accept market segmentation as truth, they zoomed out to observe how gaming fit into people's entire lives and found these gaming patterns:

- morning commutes for quick gaming sessions
- office breaks for social gaming
- evenings for family gaming
- travel-specific gaming needs

The result was the Switch—a hybrid that dissolved traditional gaming boundaries. It wasn't just a portable console that could dock to a TV; it merged home console with handheld device, single-player with social gaming, casual with hardcore experiences. The market validated this vision: over 152 million units sold globally, plus more than one billion games. More importantly, over 50 percent of users regularly play in both handheld and TV modes—proving Nintendo hadn't just created a successful product; it had identified a fundamental truth about how people wanted to play.

Scanning for Patterns

As the case study's implications settled, Lee found himself thinking of Grace's excitement at dinner last night about *Tears of the Kingdom*. "Nintendo's still doing it," Lee mumbled out loud in the Gardens' quiet space, deeply impressed. "Even now, when every other company is chasing better graphics and faster processors, they're asking different questions entirely."

"Just like they did with the Game Boy, the Wii, and the Switch." Ava nodded, apparently having finished her call. "They keep finding patterns that others miss because they're looking beyond the obvious metrics."

Lee turned back to his cluttered neural feeds, seeing them differently now. "We've been so focused on matching Delta's quantum processing that we've lost sight of why we build AI in the first place."

The Gardens' first light was breaking through Seattle's perpetual clouds. Through the smart glass, Lee could see early morning engineers arriving, their AR displays already active with the day's challenges.

"Look at them," Ava suggested. "What patterns do you see?"

Lee watched as team members clustered in small groups, sharing neural feeds, gesturing at invisible displays. Despite the technical sophistication, these moments were fundamentally human—people seeking connection, understanding, growth.

"We've been optimizing for processing power," he said slowly, the weight of revelation in his voice, "when we should be optimizing for human potential." The words felt right in a way that none of his seventeen presentations had.

The Gardens' biometric sensors registered his dropping stress levels. Sometimes clarity didn't come from cutting through the chaos but from finally understanding what the chaos was trying to tell you.

Ava nodded, bringing up their original chaos visualization. "The noise isn't something to filter out—it's something to analyze. When we zoom out, we can see patterns in what others dismiss as chaos. These patterns lead us to the real signals of opportunity."

"Like learning a new language," Lee mused, seeing how his understanding was evolving. "At first, everything sounds like meaningless noise. But gradually, you begin to recognize patterns, then words, then full sentences."

"Exactly." Ava smiled. "That's what developing Change Fluency is all about. Just as language fluency allows you to understand complex conversations without conscious translation, pattern recognition helps you navigate disruption with confidence rather than confusion. You're not just surviving chaos. You're reading it, interpreting it, finding meaning in it."

Lee's neural display pinged with another crisis alert, but this time he didn't immediately react. Instead, he thought about Nintendo's journey from playing cards to gaming empire. They hadn't just changed their technology; they'd evolved their understanding of human engagement.

"I need to completely rework this board presentation," he decided. "Instead of defending our current position, we need to show them a different future—one where AI enhances human connection rather than just processing data."

"Ready to face the board?" Ava asked, as the morning sun finally broke through.

Lee nodded, thinking of his father's words about confusion leading to clarity. "Time to help them zoom out before we zoom in."

Through the Gardens' smart glass, Seattle's tech corridor was coming alive with activity. Somewhere in those buildings, Delta's quantum processors were setting new performance records. But as Lee prepared for the board meeting, he felt something he hadn't experienced since the crisis began: purpose. Artemis might not win the processing race, but perhaps they could change the game entirely.

Principle 1: Zoom Out to Zoom In

Before diving into solutions, step back to see
the patterns in the chaos that others miss.

Key Takeaways & Considerations

Zoom Out to Analyze the Noise, Zoom In to Identify the Signal

Nintendo's success teaches us something crucial about innovation: The noise isn't something to filter out—it's something to analyze. When we zoom out, we can see patterns in what others dismiss as chaos. These patterns lead us to the real signals of opportunity.

When teams are out of focus, the natural instinct is to cut through the noise. But what if the noise itself contains the very signals we need to detect? Like a photographer adjusting their lens to first capture the entire scene before focusing on a singular subject, leaders must

- widen their aperture to take in the full landscape,

- study patterns in what others dismiss as chaos,

- look for connections between seemingly unrelated trends, and

- zoom in only after understanding the broader context.

The key is the sequence. First, zoom out to see the full landscape of noise. Study it. Look for patterns. Only then can you zoom in on the meaningful signals that others miss.

Core Principles

- The noise isn't interference; it's where the most valuable signals hide. Nintendo saw opportunity in businessmen playing with calculators while competitors focused on gaming technology.

- Innovation comes from studying patterns others dismiss as chaos. Consider how Nintendo's research into non-gamers' daily lives revealed opportunities that market research about gamers missed.

- The wider your perspective, the clearer the signal becomes. Nintendo's success with the Switch came from observing how gaming fits into people's *entire* lives.

- True focus isn't about eliminating noise but understanding it. Like Yamauchi in the Magnavox factory, sometimes the "distractions" (like watching people's reactions) contain the most valuable insights.

Practical Applications

Before Your Next Big Decision: When facing major decisions, start by listing all the "noise" you might be tempted to filter out. Consider what patterns this apparent chaos might reveal about underlying opportunities or challenges. Look beyond your immediate situation to understand the broader context that might influence your choice. Just as Nintendo saw beyond immediate gaming trends to understand deeper human needs, examine how your decision fits into larger patterns of change.

When Facing Market Disruption: Study beyond your immediate industry, just as Nintendo gained insights from watching calculator users. Observe how people actually behave rather than relying solely on what they say they want. Question industry assumptions about what "must" be true. Look for patterns in unexpected places, as these often reveal opportunities others miss while focused on traditional metrics.

For Team Leadership: Create dedicated space for broader observation before narrowing focus to specific solutions. Encourage team members to share seemingly irrelevant observations that might reveal important patterns. Practice asking "Why?" about established practices to uncover hidden assumptions and opportunities. Foster an environment where zooming out to see the bigger picture is valued as much as diving into details.

Like Nintendo's journey from playing cards to video games, your biggest opportunities might lie in the patterns others fail to see.

Put It into Practice: Scan for Signals

In today's rapidly changing business environment, leaders often miss crucial opportunities because they're too focused on immediate challenges. How do we develop the skill of pattern recognition by practicing both broad observation and focused analysis? Like a photographer adjusting their lens, you'll learn to zoom out to capture the full landscape before focusing on specific opportunities.

Scan the QR code or head over to changefluency.com/bookresources to get the downloadable **Scan for Signals** exercise.

6

Evolve
Your Vision

That's Not How We Do Things Around Here

Lee stared beyond his Coffeeholic cold brew as Artemis team members strolled past in his periphery. The past few days had shown him a hard truth: Their challenge wasn't just technical—it was perceptual. His team wasn't just defending their code; they were clinging to a way of seeing the world that no longer served them.

"But that's not how we do things around here," Mikey, a senior engineer who had reported to Sarah, said for what felt like the hundredth time. "Sarah would have approached things differently. Our existing architecture has served us well for years. Why would we completely reimagine it now?"

The second chain of change, Comfort with the Status Quo, had revealed itself. But unlike the first chain, Clutter and Chaos, this one couldn't be broken through better organization or clearer priorities. This chain required something more fundamental: a transformation in how they saw possibility itself.

"The problem isn't that we can't see the future," Ava had told him earlier that week. "It's that we're trying to view it through the lens of the past."

She was right. Every time his team discussed innovation, they started with what they knew, what they'd built, what had worked before. It was like trying to imagine flight while refusing to look up from the ground.

This wasn't just about embracing change. It was about evolving their entire vision. Ava had jotted on the whiteboard a mindset shift crucial to the second Innovation Principle:

Mindset shift from comfort with the status quo → **desire to grow**

Innovation Principle 2: Evolve Your Vision

Comfort with the Status Quo wasn't simply about resistance to change, Lee realized. It was about the coziness of familiar viewpoints, the safety of established perspectives, the security of known horizons. To break this chain, the teams needed to do more than change their processes; they needed to blast beyond the familiar.

"Because that's what we've always done," Lee started, then stopped. The words felt hollow, even to him. He glanced at his neural display, where Delta's latest numbers floated like accusatory specters: 325 million users and climbing.

His AR glasses pinged with an incoming message from Ava: "Gardens. Now. Bring your frustration."

Fresh Eyes in the Executive Suite

The Gardens were quieter than usual, although Lee spotted a few team members scattered at the large light-oak desks. Their noise-canceling headphones threw up an invisible barrier and their noses were buried in their laptops, creating a contemplative atmosphere.

"Want to hear about a moment that fundamentally changed how I think about organizational transformation?" Ava asked Lee as he walked up and she settled into her familiar spot. The afternoon light filtered through the rain-streaked panels, creating an almost ethereal atmosphere.

Lee nodded, grateful for any insight that might help break his team's resistance to change.

"Back in the early 1980s, Nintendo was facing a crisis," Ava began. "They had thousands of unsold arcade cabinets gathering dust in warehouses—a game called *Radar Scope* that had bombed in the American market. The company was burning cash, and they needed a hit to survive."

She gestured, bringing up historical footage on the Gardens' ambient display. "Most executives would have pulled their star designers to fix the problem. But Nintendo's president, Hiroshi Yamauchi, made a decision that seemed baffling at the time. He gave the assignment to Shigeru Miyamoto: a young artist with no programming experience who had originally been hired to design the company's arcade cabinets."

"Wait, he wasn't even a game designer?" Lee asked, surprised.

"Not at all. He was essentially the company's industrial artist—the person who made the cabinets look nice. He had never created a game before," Ava explained. "The established game designers were horrified. Why trust their company's future to someone so inexperienced?"

The Gardens' displays shifted to show early sketches of what would become one of the most iconic characters in gaming history.

"But Miyamoto approached the problem differently. Instead of focusing on technical specifications like the other designers, he started with a story. He imagined a character—a carpenter with a girlfriend and a pet—who had to rescue the girlfriend from a gorilla."

"*Donkey Kong*!" Lee yelled, causing a few workers to look up.

"Exactly. While experienced designers were creating space shooters and racing games, Miyamoto created the first game with a true narrative structure. He broke every convention, and the result was revolutionary. *Donkey Kong* saved Nintendo from bankruptcy and launched what would become the most successful franchise in gaming history."

"But that's just one lucky break," Lee pointed out. "Taking a risk on an outsider worked once, but—"

"It wasn't just once," Ava interrupted. "Yamauchi institutionalized this approach. He repeatedly looked for talent in unexpected places and gave newcomers the freedom to challenge assumptions. When Nintendo needed a breakthrough portable device, they turned to Gunpei Yokoi, an engineer who had started as a maintenance worker. His Game Boy went on to sell over 118 million units."

Lee considered this. "So, fresh eyes weren't just tolerated. They were actively sought out."

"Exactly. Nintendo created what they called 'lateral thinking with withered technology': finding new approaches using established tools. But the real innovation was in whose voices they valued. They deliberately elevated perspectives from outside their established hierarchy."

Lee thought about his own team structure, where seniority often determined whose ideas got priority.

Companies that thrive can fluidly shift between viewpoints, **bringing fresh eyes to old problems and experienced wisdom to new challenges.**

"There's a beautiful Japanese concept called *shoshin:* beginner's mind," Ava continued. "It means approaching problems without preconceptions, as a beginner would. Yamauchi understood that sometimes the person with the least experience has the freshest perspective.

"You know what they say about likable leaders getting more done," Ava mused, eyeing Lee with a mischievous grin. "Which is probably why you've been struggling so much lately." Lee's mock offense was met with Ava's laugh—somehow both gentle and merciless at the same time.

"But how do you actually implement something like that?" Lee asked. "We can't just put junior team members in charge of everything."

"That's not what Nintendo did either," Ava replied. "They created systems where experience and fresh perspective could collaborate. Miyamoto was paired with experienced engineers who helped execute his vision. But the vision itself came from someone who wasn't constrained by 'how we've always done things.'

"The most adaptable organizations develop what linguists call 'code-switching'—the ability to shift between different communication styles as the situation demands. Developing fluency in vision-casting works the same way, allowing leaders to see opportunities through various frameworks and adapt their approach accordingly."

"Vision-casting..." Lee reflected, beginning to see the connection to their broader transformation efforts. "Not just having a static view of what's possible, but being able to shift perspectives as needed—seeing through the eyes of a beginner when we need fresh ideas or through the lens of experience when we need execution."

"Exactly." Ava nodded. "Vision-casting. The companies that thrive aren't just comfortable with one way of seeing;

they can fluidly shift between different viewpoints, bringing fresh eyes to old problems and experienced wisdom to new challenges."

Lee glanced at his neural display calendar and groaned audibly.

"Something wrong?" Ava asked.

"I've got three consecutive two-hour meetings about our new meeting structure, followed by a meeting to plan next week's meetings about reducing meeting time," Lee replied, rubbing his temples. "The irony is we'll probably run out of time and have to schedule a follow-up meeting to finish discussing how to have fewer meetings."

Ava snorted. "Ah, the corporate circle of life. Nothing says productivity like twelve people watching someone share their screen while trying to find the right document."

Vision-Casting: A Ten-Star Revolution

Ava shifted in her chair, her energy building. "Before you go, let me share another story that changed how I think about vision and possibility. A few years back, Brian Chesky, Airbnb's CEO, was speaking to a class at Stanford's Graduate School of Business. He posed a simple question that would revolutionize how we think about customer experience."

She brought up a new visualization in the air between them. "Chesky explained how with services like Uber or Airbnb, a five-star rating usually just means nothing bad happened. It's the absence of problems, not the presence of magic. So, he had asked his team: What would a six-star experience look like?"

The visualization began to build, star by star. "A six-star experience meant arriving to find a bottle of wine, fresh fruit, a handwritten note. Seven stars? A limo picks you up from the airport, and there's a dedicated experience matching your interests. Eight stars? You arrive to find an elephant and a parade in your honor. Nine stars? The Beatles reunite to perform at your check-in. And ten stars?"

"Let me guess," Lee interjected, "something involving space?"

"Exactly!" Ava laughed. "Elon shows up and takes you to space. Now, obviously, they couldn't implement the more outrageous ideas. But that wasn't the point. The exercise freed people's minds from the constraints of current reality. It gave them permission to imagine beyond incremental improvements."

"And it worked?"

"In less than ten years, they achieved the entire growth of Hilton, a company that had been operating for over a century. But more importantly, they transformed how people think about travel and belonging. They didn't just compete with hotels; they reimagined what hospitality could mean."

The Implementation

The next morning, Lee stood before his team again, but this time with a different approach. He'd arranged the conference room differently, with junior developers and interns seated prominently at the table instead of in their usual spots along the wall.

"Today, we're going to do something different," he announced. "We're not here to discuss how we've always done things. We're here to imagine what might be possible if we started fresh."

He shared both the Miyamoto *Donkey Kong* story and the ten-star exercise, watching as expressions shifted from skepticism to curiosity. Then, he posed a simple question: "What would our platform look like if we built it for 2050, not 2035?"

Raj, a junior developer who usually stayed quiet in meetings but was now sitting at the table, raised his hand tentatively. "What if we stopped thinking about our AI as a tool and started thinking about it as a creative partner? Like, imagine if it could not just assist but actually collaborate in real-time with users..."

The room fell silent, but this time with possibility rather than resistance. Lee caught Maya Chen, VP of Operations, who had come to observe, actually taking notes.

For the next two hours, they mapped out increasingly ambitious visions, each building on the last. The energy in the room was electric, reminding Lee of his daughter Grace's excitement about her science fair project: that pure, unbridled enthusiasm for what might be possible.

Maya leaned over to Lee as the junior team members excitedly debated. "Remember when we thought innovation meant adding more features?" she whispered.

"Yeah." Lee chuckled. "Like putting racing stripes on a horse and calling it a Ferrari."

Maya snorted her Coffeeholic cold brew through her nose, drawing curious stares. "Worth it," she muttered, dabbing at her shirt with a napkin.

The Breakthrough

As the session wound down, Raj cleared his throat. "You know what I think Delta got wrong?" The room turned to look at him. "They're so focused on individual AI capabilities; they've missed the bigger picture. What if we built something that helped teams think better together? Not just individual productivity but collective intelligence?"

Lee felt a familiar tingle of excitement—the same he'd felt when he'd first joined Artemis. This wasn't just a product insight; it was a vision that could reshape their entire approach.

Later that evening, back in the Gardens with Ava, Lee shared the day's breakthrough. "It's amazing what happens when you create space for new voices," he reflected.

Ava smiled. "That's the thing about vision: It doesn't just evolve, it expands. When you include more perspectives, you see possibilities you never could have imagined alone."

"Like the Wright brothers seeing beyond bicycles to flight," Lee mused.

"Exactly." Ava nodded. "Speaking of which, ready to try something really ambitious tomorrow? I think it's time we invited some actual users into these discussions…"

Through the Gardens' glass panels, the Seattle skyline emerged from the clearing storm. Somewhere out there, Delta was still growing, still innovating. But despite that, Lee felt emotionally calm.

The chain of Comfort with the Status Quo hadn't been broken exactly, but it had been transformed into something else: a launching pad for imagination.

Principle 2: Evolve Your Vision

Fresh perspectives and unconventional viewpoints often
lead to the breakthroughs your organization needs.

Key Takeaways & Considerations

- Vision evolution requires diverse perspectives and voices.

- Breaking from "how we've always done things" starts with giving people permission to imagine.

- True innovation comes from creating space for all voices to contribute.

- The best breakthroughs often come from unexpected sources.

- Transformation requires both the courage to speak and courage to listen.

Put It into Practice: Ten-Star Experience

Ready to break free from "just good enough," apply incremental thinking, and imagine transformative possibilities?

Download the **Ten-Star Experience** worksheet at changefluency.com/bookresources or scan the QR code.

From the Field
Mars Inc.— Evolving Vision Through Principle

WHEN FRANK MARS began making buttercream candies in his Tacoma, Washington, kitchen in 1911, he couldn't have envisioned that his small operation would evolve into a $45-billion global enterprise spanning chocolate, pet care, food, and health care. What makes Mars remarkable isn't just its growth but how it has continuously evolved its vision while maintaining unwavering commitment to its founding principles.

Beyond the Status Quo

Most century-old companies become entrenched in "how we've always done things," but Mars has repeatedly demonstrated the courage to evolve beyond its comfort zone. In an industry where competitors protected established product lines and familiar markets, Mars repeatedly asked, "What could we become?"

Forrest Mars Jr., who ran Mars with his brother John for almost three decades, frequently encouraged a "healthy dissatisfaction with the status quo." Many people think of Mars as just a chocolate company, but it doesn't feel like they ever defined themselves that way.

This mindset proved crucial when Mars made what seemed like a radical departure in the 1930s—entering the pet food business through the acquisition of Chappel Brothers, makers of Chappie dog food. At a time when the pet food industry was in its infancy, this move puzzled industry observers.

Fresh Eyes in Action

Mars's ability to evolve its vision often came from deliberately seeking fresh perspectives. Like Nintendo inviting nonprogrammers like Shigeru Miyamoto to reimagine gaming, Mars consistently elevated unexpected voices.

- In 1932, Forrest Mars Sr. (Frank's son) returned from Europe with fresh eyes and a revolutionary idea—candy-coated chocolate buttons inspired by Spanish Civil War rations—that would become M&Ms.

- In the 1960s, Mars invited veterinarians and animal nutritionists to influence product development at a time when competitors viewed pet food merely as a by-product business.

- In the 1970s, while most companies kept sustainability initiatives within PR departments, Mars invited environmental scientists into core strategy discussions, evolving its vision decades before *sustainability* became a business buzzword.

John Pfahlert, a former Mars executive, explained: "The Mars family has always understood that vision stagnates when the same people are in the room. They're masterful at bringing in perspectives that challenge comfortable assumptions."

Ten-Star Vision Exercise in Practice

Decades before Airbnb's ten-star experience exercise became a business school case study, Mars was already practicing a similar approach to visioning. When entering new categories, they wouldn't just ask what an improved product looked like—they imagined what a transformative product could be.

When developing Pedigree dog food in the 1950s, they didn't ask, "How can we make better dog food?" Instead, they asked, "What if dog food could actually contribute to a dog's health and longevity?" This evolved vision led to breakthroughs in pet nutrition that transformed the industry.

Similarly, in the 1990s when Mars evolved its vision of chocolate from mere confection to premium experience through the development of high-end brands like Dove, it wasn't just creating better chocolate; it was reimagining the category itself.

Evolution Without Abandonment

What makes Mars's approach to evolving vision particularly instructive is how they balance evolution with continuity. While they've repeatedly reinvented what they could become, they've never abandoned their five principles: quality, responsibility, mutuality, efficiency, and freedom.

Most companies make the mistake of thinking evolution means replacement. But the truth is that its principles were the constant that allowed Mars to evolve everything else with confidence. "[Our five] principles are the glue that holds us together," explained Victoria Mars, part of the fourth generation of the family involved with the company.

This approach proved invaluable when Mars made its largest evolution leap in 2008: the $23-billion acquisition of Wrigley. Rather than forcing Wrigley to adopt Mars's ways of working, they allowed both visions to inform each other, creating something stronger than either could have achieved alone.

Application for Organizations

For leaders seeking to evolve the vision of their organizations beyond comfortable patterns, Mars offers three pivotal practices:

1 **Principles Over Prescription:** Establish clear principles that provide guidance without dictating specific outcomes. Mars's five principles create a framework for evolution rather than a formula for replication.

2 **Outsider Integration:** Systematically incorporate perspectives from outside your core expertise. Mars regularly brings scientific, cultural, and even competitive perspectives into vision-setting exercises.

3 **Generational Thinking:** Frame vision evolution across decades, not quarters. Mars's private ownership allows it to evolve gradually rather than through disruptive pivots, creating more sustainable transformation.

Mars's journey from simple candymaker to global enterprise wasn't driven by abandoning its heritage but by continuously evolving its vision of what that heritage could become. In your own transformation efforts, consider how you might follow the Mars example—not by rejecting your past but by imagining greater possibilities for your future while honoring the principles that define your organization's character.

7
Work in Wonder

Tumors and Building Blocks

As the afternoon sun filtered through Lee's kitchen window, it caught dust motes swirling above the kitchen island counter, where his neural interface was projecting the day's metrics in soft blue light. Working from home, Lee found the house quiet except for the gentle hum of the refrigerator and occasional neighborhood noises filtering through, a stark contrast to the Gardens' ambient systems.

In that moment, the neural interface buzzed with an alert, its clinical blue glow seeming to pulse with his heartbeat: "Medical Report Available: Urgent Review Required." Lee caught his own reflection in the kitchen window, the glare rendering his image ghostly and uncertain.

Working on autopilot, he reached for a soft chocolate chip cookie from the pantry. But nothing could soften the words that materialized before him: "3-mm tumor detected in pituitary gland, located directly beneath brain."

Lee absentmindedly unfolded the transparent wrap enveloping the cookie, glancing around for a saving grace. His eyes fell on the family photos magnetized to his refrigerator. Grace's science fair ribbon beside a crayon drawing by Audrey. The juxtaposition of his work crisis and family life hit him suddenly—both feel precariously balanced.

I'm going to die.

The thought crashed through him with a physical force, drowning out the gentle hum of the refrigerator. His mind desperately jumped to Teresa. Grace. Audrey. What he would give to see them grow up together. What would they do without him? All of it suddenly fragile, uncertain.

"Tumor currently benign," the report continued dispassionately. "Monitoring required. Risk of complications if growth occurs."

I'm only forty-two. This can't be happening. Not now. Not with everything at stake with Delta, with the team counting on me, with my kids...

"Your cortisol levels indicate severe distress," Lee's ambient AI noted with artificial concern. "Initiating calming protocols."

The neutral interface began its programmed response—subtle shifts in haptic nudges, a gentle modulation to massage Lee's temple—but Lee barely noticed. His analytical mind, the same one that had helped him navigate countless technical challenges at Artemis, now turned traitor, spinning out worst-case scenarios with ruthless efficiency.

His display pinged with another notification.

Ava appeared. She took one look at his face and stopped dead in her tracks.

"Lee?" The usual confidence in her voice was replaced with immediate concern.

"I..." His voice cracked. He'd faced board meetings, market crashes, technical crises... but this was different. This was primal.

Lee gestured shakily, sharing his medical display. "They found a tumor. Right here." He pointed to his head, his finger trembling slightly. "Three millimeters. The doctor sent it in an email, can you believe that? Just a note about how there's a half percent chance this thing kills me."

His voice cracked on the last word. "Point five percent. I've spent my entire career working with probabilities, Ava. I know it's a small number. I should be relieved. But all I can think about is Grace and Audrey growing up without…" He couldn't finish the sentence.

Unimaginable

Lee stared out his window. A cloud had rolled over Lake Union, a float plane landing in the darkening blue water that had just lost its shimmer, pushing out gray waves on the other side of an apparent turbulent landing.

Ava paused, holding the silence for a moment, honoring the weight of his fear before asking, "What's going through your mind?"

"Everything," Lee admitted, running his hands through his hair. "Every possible outcome, every scenario. My mind won't stop spinning through probabilities. Point five percent becomes 100 percent when it's your tumor, your kids, your life." He stared in a daze at his marble kitchen island, its usual calming pattern now seeming to mirror his anxiety. "I keep trying to control it through analysis, but…"

"But some things can't be controlled through spreadsheets," Ava finished softly. She settled into the chair at the Gardens, a signal that she was there to offer support but giving him space to process. "You know what this reminds me of?"

Ava's question caught him off guard. In the office, surrounded by the Gardens' ambient systems, it would be easier to maintain the professional facade. But here, standing in his kitchen with his children's artwork as backdrop, the compartmentalization felt impossible.

Lee stared at her, almost angry at how calmly she was taking this. "You're about to tell me this is another leadership lesson, aren't you? That this is some kind of growth opportunity?"

"No," Ava said, her voice gentle but firm. "Right now, this is about you facing something terrifying. But it does remind me of another organization that faced its own mortality: LEGO."

"LEGO?" Lee's incredulity cut through his fear for a moment. "The toy company? This isn't about plastic bricks, Ava. This is about . . . "

" . . . life and death?" Ava finished. "In 2003, LEGO was dying. Not metaphorically—they were losing $1 million a day. Their entire world was being disrupted by digital entertainment. Everyone said physical toys were obsolete. The numbers, the trends, the analysis: Everything pointed to their extinction."

Outside, the ripples from the float plane landing had subdued, easing back into the calm, natural ebb and flow, as Ava continued. "They tried everything you're doing now: analyzing probabilities, running scenarios, seeking certainty. But that approach nearly killed them faster."

"What saved them?" Lee asked, despite himself.

"They discovered something profound about uncertainty," Ava replied. "The same thing I need to show you now." She gestured to the Gardens' display interface. "Show me the Cone of Possibilities framework."

The Cone of Possibilities

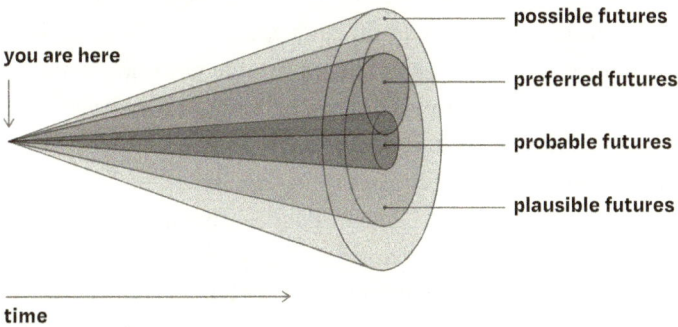

As Lee leaned on his kitchen island, the air between them filled with a geometric visualization: a cone expanding from a single point into multiple branching pathways, creating an immersive experience of expanding possibility.

The Cone of Possibilities

you are here

possible futures

preferred futures

probable futures

plausible futures

time

"In design strategy and futures thinking," Ava explained, her voice kind but purposeful, "a professor, Joseph Voros, developed the Cone of Possibilities to move beyond binary thinking. As futurists and designers ruminate on scenario planning, they use the Cone of Possibilities to suspend disbelief and unlock their imaginations. It is helpful to balance *what's present* and *what's possible*. Right now, your mind is fixed on a single question: 'Will I die?' But that's just one possible future among many."

She gestured, and the holographic cone expanded, its pathways multiplying. "Let's look at different types of futures. First, there are possible futures—everything that could theoretically happen, even if unlikely. Then, there are plausible futures—what might realistically occur given what we know. Probable futures are what's likely to happen based on current trends. And finally, there are preferred futures—what we actively want to create."

"You know what's interesting about both language learning and facing uncertainty?" Ava asked. "In both cases, those who embrace ambiguity progress faster than those who demand certainty."

She brought up research on language acquisition. "Studies show that successful language learners have high 'ambiguity tolerance'; they're comfortable not understanding everything, making mistakes, existing in the space between knowledge and uncertainty. They don't need to master every rule before attempting conversation."

Ava gestured to the Cone of Possibilities still hovering between them. "Developing Change Fluency requires the same comfort with ambiguity. It's about building the capacity to navigate the unknown without needing perfect information—to wonder rather than worry when facing uncertainty."

Lee thought about his medical diagnosis and Delta's market moves, two profound uncertainties he was struggling to navigate. "So, wondering isn't just philosophical. It's practical," he said slowly. "It's developing the mental flexibility to operate effectively even without complete understanding."

"Exactly." Ava smiled. "And like language fluency, it deepens with practice. Each time you choose curiosity over certainty, you're building your Change Fluency, your capacity to navigate disruption as opportunity rather than threat."

The visual display began mirroring these pathways as Ava continued. "Instead of fixating on that 0.5 percent possibility, let's explore other futures. What's probable based on the medical data?"

Lee took a shaky breath. "Statistically... probable means the tumor remains stable. Most pituitary tumors grow slowly or not at all."

"Good. Now, what's plausible?"

"Regular monitoring catches any changes early. I build a team of specialists. I modify my lifestyle: better sleep, no alcohol, more exercise..." Lee's analytical mind had begun engaging differently with the uncertainty.

"And preferred?" Ava prompted softly.

"I live a long, healthy life. I see my kids grow up. I use this wake-up call to become more present, more intentional." Lee's voice grew stronger. "I build a care plan that lets me focus on what matters: family, purpose, impact."

The Cone's patterns shifted again, each possibility creating new branches of light.

Lee stood abruptly, pacing before the kitchen island. "But there are things I can control, right? I mean, I've already decided—no more drinking. Those occasional gin and tonics on Fridays? Gone. I'm prioritizing eight hours of sleep, even though with the Delta crisis..." He ran his hands through his hair again. "I'll even bring back basketball and squash into my weekly routine."

Ava watched him, a smile playing at her lips. "Those are good changes. But notice something? You're still trying to control everything, optimize every variable. What if God has different plans for you, beyond anything you could predict, something completely unexpected?"

Lee stopped pacing, struck by the question.

"What if," Ava continued, "this moment isn't just about survival—it's about sitting with your fear, in the uncertainty of it all?

"You see wonder isn't about ignoring reality. It's about engaging with all of reality, not just our fears. LEGO didn't just avoid bankruptcy; they discovered new ways of

It's helpful to balance *what's present* and *what's possible.*

thinking about play itself. They went from asking 'Will we survive?' to 'What other possibilities are out there?'"

"This sounds good in theory," Lee said, "but I feel like it's so tough to live in that space of possibility without going crazy from uncertainty."

Ava leaned forward. "You create concrete action plans for each type of future. For the *probable* future of ongoing monitoring, you research the best specialists and imaging centers. For the *plausible* future of lifestyle changes, you start building new habits now—I know a great sleep specialist who works with tech executives. For the *preferred* future of a long, healthy life, you begin restructuring your priorities, many of which you have started to identify now. Each pathway needs its own strategy."

Over in the Gardens, Ava moved to the digital whiteboard and began projecting onto Lee's augmented display. "This brings us to the third Innovation Principle," she said, her marker gliding across the surface as she wrote:

Mindset shift from seeking certainty → **embracing curiosity**

Innovation Principle 3: Work in Wonder

"Most organizations—and most leaders—face uncertainty the same way you initially faced your diagnosis," Ava explained. "They try to control it through analysis, to eliminate it through data. But true innovation, like genuine healing, requires something else entirely: the courage to wonder."

The words hung in the air between them as Lee considered their weight. His instinct as VP of Product had always been to seek certainty—in specifications, in metrics, in outcomes. Now, facing both personal mortality and organizational disruption, he was being asked to embrace something fundamentally different.

"In the age of artificial intelligence and quantum computing," Ava continued, "everyone has access to the same data, the same analysis, the same certainties. The difference-maker isn't who has the most precise predictions; it's who has the capacity to wonder about what those predictions miss."

The smart glass on Lee's fridge suddenly flashed with another alert: "BREAKING: Delta Tech Announces Quantum AI Breakthrough. Stock Impact Predicted -28%."

Lee felt the familiar grip of panic, but this time it was different. The personal and professional uncertainties seemed to merge, creating a moment of profound vulnerability—and possibility.

"Look," Ava said, gesturing to both his medical readout and the alert about Delta. "Two uncertainties, two invitations to wonder. The question isn't whether you'll face them, but how."

Beyond the smart glass, it had begun to rain. As millions of raindrops scattered across Lake Union's surface, Lee couldn't help but appreciate the beauty in the ripples being created, the lake being transformed into a canvas of possibilities.

"And here's what makes LEGO's transformation so remarkable," Ava said, her eyes lighting up. "They didn't just survive by abandoning their status quo—they thrived by reimagining it. Instead of seeing digital technology as a threat to physical play, they wondered about new possibilities. What if digital and physical could enhance each other? What if their precise manufacturing could enable new forms of creativity? What if their deep understanding of play could inform new ways of learning? What if there was something else—outside of just toys, like movies?"

At the Gardens, Ava's display shifted to show LEGO's transformation across multiple pivots:

- **Mindstorms:** First came Mindstorms in 1998, their revolutionary robotics platform that merged physical bricks with digital programming. Rather than seeing technology as a threat to traditional play, LEGO used it to enhance creativity. The platform went beyond teaching coding—it showed how digital and physical experiences could amplify each other.

- **Marvel:** Then came their strategic partnership with Marvel in 2009, transforming LEGO from a toy company into a storytelling powerhouse. While competitors chased digital entertainment, LEGO realized that modern play wasn't about choosing between physical and digital—it was about connecting them. The Marvel LEGO sets were gateways to imagination that bridged movies, games, and traditional play.

- **Movies:** LEGO's entry into movies proved especially transformative. *The LEGO Movie* in 2014 went beyond entertainment: It reimagined what a toy company could be. By celebrating creativity and poking fun at rigid thinking (through characters like President Business), LEGO turned its own near-bankruptcy story into a blockbuster message about the power of imagination.

- **Education:** Their education initiatives revealed perhaps the deepest insight: In a digital age, physical play becomes more valuable, not less. LEGO Education's expansion into STEAM learning showed how hands-on experimentation could teach complex concepts better than screens alone. LEGO wasn't only making toys anymore; it was also shaping how future generations would learn and create.

"Each pivot built on LEGO's core strength," Ava explained, "of understanding how people play while expanding what play could mean in a changing world. Like Nintendo with the Switch, LEGO not only survived disruption, they used it to discover new possibilities for their core mission.

"They broke free from their chain of comfort not by rejecting their past but by wondering about their future. And that's exactly what both you and Artemis need to do now."

Lee's AR display nudged him with an update on Delta's market data, bringing him back to the present. "So, how do we actually do this?" he asked. "I have a TechMinds team that can't wait to just quit. How do we shift the team's comfort with the status quo to get them working in wonder? They're so proud of what they've built that anytime I bring up integration, they feel like I'm just taking it away from them."

Ava just smiled. "I wonder too."

Principle 3: Work in Wonder

Curiosity about multiple possibilities will unlock a level of innovation that certainty-seeking would never discover.

Key Takeaways & Considerations

How do we lead others through uncertainty when we're still finding our own way? Wonder isn't about ignoring uncertainty; it's about engaging with all possibilities. When we shift from seeking certainty to embracing wonder, we unlock new paths for innovation and growth.

The Cone of Possibilities Framework

Possible Futures:	**Plausible** Futures:
Everything that could theoretically happen lives in this space, unconstrained by current limitations or practical concerns. These futures represent our boldest imaginings and most radical possibilities, serving as a source for breakthrough thinking even if they seem impossible today.	Within the realm of what might realistically occur given our current capabilities and constraints, these futures balance ambition with achievability, helping organizations stretch beyond immediate limitations while remaining grounded in practical possibility.
Probable Futures:	**Preferred** Futures:
Based on current trends and existing data, these futures represent what's likely to happen if present patterns continue. Understanding probable futures helps organizations prepare for immediate challenges while identifying opportunities to shape different outcomes.	These are the futures we actively want to create, aligned with our values and vision. They represent not just what could happen or what's likely to happen but what we want to happen based on our deepest aspirations and commitments.

Key Principles

Embracing Uncertainty: Rather than trying to eliminate uncertainty through analysis, successful organizations learn to use it as a catalyst for innovation. Like a sailor using wind conditions to power their journey, leaders can harness uncertainty to drive exploration and discovery of new possibilities.

Leading Through Ambiguity: Effective leadership in uncertain times requires balancing vulnerability with vision. By sharing both concerns and hopes openly while maintaining focus on possibility, leaders create environments where teams feel safe exploring unknown territory together.

Questions to Consider: Wonder opens doors that certainty keeps closed. By regularly asking "What if..." and "How might we..." organizations keep themselves open to possibilities that pure analysis might miss, creating space for breakthrough innovations that transcend current limitations.

Put It into Practice: The Cone of Possibilities

When facing uncertainty, our natural instinct is to seek binary outcomes—success or failure, growth or decline, survival or extinction. Instead of trying to predict a single future, explore multiple scenarios through the **Cone of Possibilities** exercise to reveal opportunities and pathways you might otherwise miss.

Head on over to changefluency.com/bookresources or scan the QR Code to get started.

Reminder: You can chat with JAI (Jay AI) on any of the exercises to get coaching on your personal business challenge!

From the Field
Spotify's Strategic Navigation of Possibility

WHEN SPOTIFY LAUNCHED in 2008, the music industry was struggling in the wake of digital disruption. Record
labels faced declining revenue, artists questioned traditional distribution models, and consumers increasingly
turned to illegal downloads.

Most companies were trapped in binary thinking: either
defend the traditional ownership model or surrender to digital chaos.

Into this chaos stepped Swedish entrepreneurs Daniel
Ek and Martin Lorentzon with a radical proposition: What
if music could be free, legal, and instantly accessible?

Spotify found a different path by systematically exploring multiple futures—demonstrating how organizations can
use the Cone of Possibilities as a strategic tool.

Applying the Cone of Possibilities

Imagine Spotify's leadership team gathered around a whiteboard around 2006, mapping out their strategy using a framework similar to the Cone of Possibilities.

Possible Futures (Exploration Phase): The team explored radical possibilities: What if all music could be instantly accessible to everyone? What if artists could reach fans directly without traditional gatekeepers? What if listening patterns could be tracked to create personalized experiences that would transform music discovery?

Plausible Futures (Constraining Phase): They examined realistic constraints: Given licensing requirements, how could they balance accessibility with legal compliance? Within existing technology limitations, what streaming quality was achievable? How might they create a sustainable business without alienating either artists or listeners?

Probable Futures (Reality Testing Phase): The team assessed likely outcomes. Based on early user testing, what features would drive adoption? Given music industry resistance, which labels might be early adopters? How would different pricing models affect user behavior in various markets?

Preferred Futures (Strategic Choice Phase): After evaluating options, they made strategic commitments. They would pursue a freemium model with both advertising and subscription tiers. They would focus on user experience first, negotiating with labels second. They would prioritize catalog breadth over initial profitability to build the critical mass needed for success.

Learning Through Iteration

As Spotify launched and grew, the team continually cycled through this framework to navigate emerging challenges. When artists complained about royalties, they explored new possibilities like direct uploads and promotional tools. When competitors emerged with exclusive content, they developed podcast offerings and expanded beyond music.

Rather than becoming paralyzed by uncertainty or jumping to conclusions, Spotify maintained a dynamic relationship with possibility: constantly exploring, testing, adapting, and committing.

By 2024, this approach had transformed the industry in ways few had imagined possible. According to its "Loud & Clear" transparency report in March 2025, Spotify paid out a record $10 billion to the music industry in 2024 alone—the largest single-year payout by any retailer in music history. Moreover, nearly 1,500 artists generated over $1 million in royalties from Spotify alone that year, with 80 percent of these artists never reaching the Global Daily Top 50 chart, proving that sustainable success no longer requires chart-topping hits.

By embracing wonder rather than demanding certainty, Spotify transformed how people experience music. The framework they implicitly used—similar to our Cone of Possibilities—offers a template for how organizations can navigate through disruption while maintaining both vision and flexibility.

8
Emergency

What a Cluster

"Without Sarah's architecture, we've had to rethink our entire approach to integration."

The emergency integration meeting with TechMinds was imploding on itself. It had barely started five minutes ago, but it was already off the rails. The Gardens' biometric sensors had detected elevated stress patterns across both teams, their data visualizations pulsing with warning indicators on the smart glass panels.

Red and orange clusters showed mounting tension in both Seattle and Bangalore, with particular hot spots around the core development teams.

Lee didn't know what to do with the TechMinds team in front of him—acquired but not yet integrated, resistant but brilliantly innovative.

Through the windows, Seattle's eternal mist created ghostly reflections of the assembled teams: Artemis engineers in their standard dark hoodies, TechMinds developers in similarly casual clothing, all of them radiating the particular tension that came with forced collaboration. The Gardens' living walls turned a tranquil blue, their patterns attempting to ease the discord between the groups.

"Integration timelines are meaningless if we can't align on basic architecture," Rachel from TechMinds was saying, her holographic avatar projecting from Bangalore with characteristic intensity. The neural interface made her presence feel almost physical, down to the slight tremor in her hands as she gestured at architectural diagrams. "Sarah would have understood that."

Lee could feel his temper rising.

"Your infrastructure requirements are forcing us to rebuild our entire emotional recognition engine. That's months of work, completely wasted."

"Rachel, the timelines are nonnegotiable. Maybe you just need to do your job," Lee snapped.

Rachel glared him. "Excuse me? You can't talk to me like that."

Lee realized he had gone too far. The stress from finding out about his tumor was clearly materializing in an ugly way.

"You're right. I'm sorry." He backtracked quickly, embarrassed by his outburst.

Beneath the Anger

"Actually," Lee started, then stopped, his throat suddenly tight. The Gardens' ambient lighting dimmed slightly, as if giving him space. "This is no excuse, but I . . . There's something I need to share with all of you." He took a shaky breath.

"Three days ago, I . . ." His hand unconsciously moved to the spot where the tumor sat. "I received some medical news. They found a tumor. Here." He touched his head. "It's small—three millimeters. But it's in my pituitary gland, just under my brain." His voice cracked on the last word.

The room fell silent. The kind of silence that makes you aware of your own heartbeat. Even the usual hum of the neural interfaces seemed muted. That wasn't what the team was expecting to hear.

Lee stood there, hands trembling slightly. Now that he'd actually said the words out loud, they hung in the air like a weight he wasn't sure how to carry.

Through the neural interface, he could see the teams exchanging glances—Seattle to Bangalore, Artemis to Tech-Minds—their avatars shifting uncomfortably in the shared digital space. The Gardens' ambient systems dimmed further, as if sheltering this fragile moment.

"Lee?" Priya's voice was barely above a whisper, her avatar moving closer. She was the youngest member of the TechMinds team, and until now, he'd rarely heard her speak in these meetings. "My sister," she continued softly, each word careful and deliberate. "She had something similar last year. I remember how scary those first days were, when everything felt like it was falling apart."

She raised her hand tentatively.

"You don't need to raise your hand, Priya." Lee glanced around the room. "You're literally the only one speaking right now."

"In our culture, we bring food when someone is ill. Our team can send over a few different dishes for you."

Lee looked alarmed. "That's incredibly kind but—"

"Too late," Rachel interrupted with a smile. "I already scheduled the delivery drones to your house later. Hope you like spicy food."

Lee nodded gratefully at Rachel and Priya, feeling an ease wrap around him given their thoughtfulness. He took a deep breath before continuing.

"You know what Ava taught me about facing uncertainty?" He gestured to the room's holographic display. "Show Cone of Possibilities framework."

Wonder at Work

The air between them filled with the geometric visualization: a cone expanding from a single point into multiple branching pathways. The team watched the immersive experience of expanding possibility in awe.

"When we face uncertainty, whether it's personal or professional, we tend to fixate on the worst possible future. But that's just one path among many." Lee's voice grew stronger as he explained. "There are possible futures—everything that could theoretically happen. Plausible futures: what might realistically occur. Probable futures: what's likely based on current trends. And preferred futures: what we actively want to create."

Rachel's avatar leaned forward, her technical skepticism giving way to unexpected empathy. "I'm sorry you're going through this, Lee. I can't imagine what that stress must be like. Our emotional AI research... It aligns perfectly with this framework." She brought up a visualization of their data. "We've been studying how humans respond to uncertainty. Not just the surface patterns—elevated cortisol, increased neural activity in the amygdala—but the deeper adaptations. The patterns we've seen... They're not just about fear. They're about possibility."

She gestured, bringing up a visualization of their research. "When humans face uncertainty, their brains don't just activate stress responses. They create new neural pathways, new possibilities for adaptation. It's why we

Successful transformation requires being **stubborn on vision and flexible on details.**

designed our AI to recognize not only what people are feeling but also how they're evolving through those feelings."

Maya Chen, who had been silent until that point, blurted out, "That's so fascinating!" The energy in the room got a little bit lighter. She moved to the central display, pulling up her own visualization.

"Here's how we typically handle uncertainty in Operations," she explained, showing traditional risk management frameworks. "But look what happens when we overlay the emotional AI patterns Rachel's team discovered. New branches of future features appear on the product road map."

The TechMinds team, initially defensive about integration, began actively engaging with the framework. Priya, the youngest member of their team, moved to the digital whiteboard and began tagging ideas: "possible" for the wildest innovations they could imagine, "plausible" for the ones within reach, "preferred" for the solutions that felt right. The Cone of Possibilities was coming alive in their hands, transforming from theoretical framework into practical foundation.

The Gardens' systems registered unprecedented team coherence as what began as crisis management evolved into collaborative innovation. TechMinds' emotional AI capabilities combined with Artemis' infrastructure and Maya's operational rigor were creating something none of them could have built alone.

As Lee watched the teams collaborating, deep in thought, Ava entered the room. He glanced over at her, and a moment of clarity emerged: Successful transformation required being stubborn on vision and flexible on details. Their unwavering commitment to human-centered AI remained the North Star, even as they were open to reimagining how that vision would materialize. This delicate balance—holding fast to purpose while adapting the path—was the essence of leading through uncertainty.

The living walls pulsed with new patterns of possibility as teams that had once been divided now worked seamlessly across physical and digital spaces.

"You know," Ava said to Lee quietly, "at my previous company, I worked through cancer treatment during our biggest product launch. It failed because we were too insular—I was too busy 'leading' to create space for fresh perspectives."

She gestured toward the Cone of Possibilities visualization. "I've spent years teaching others to embrace uncertainty while avoiding it myself. These principles aren't just organizational tools—they're life philosophies."

"Sounds like you're thinking about making a change," Lee observed.

A smile touched Ava's lips. "Perhaps it's time I practice what I preach. Create space for wonder in my own life, not just my work."

Someone from the TechMinds team cleared their throat. "So, this is what happens when we stop fighting each other? We actually make progress?"

Maya raised an eyebrow. "Don't sound so disappointed. I had a whole PowerPoint prepared on why you were all wrong."

"Save it for next week," Rachel quipped, a hint of a smile breaking through her usually serious demeanor. "I'm sure we'll find something new to argue about by then."

Lee, leaning against a pillar, looked shocked at what was happening, barely able to recognize the teams in front of him. He couldn't help but comment to Ava, "Look at them—they're not just *working* together, they're *wondering* together."

From the Field
Shazam's
Impossible Dream

IN 1999, Chris Barton envisioned something that seemed technologically impossible: a service that could identify any song playing anywhere with just a brief audio sample. At the time, smartphones didn't exist, mobile phones had minimal computing power, and music recognition algorithms were in their infancy.

"Everyone told me it couldn't be done," Barton recalled. "The technology wasn't there. The phones weren't powerful enough. The algorithms would require supercomputers." The obstacles were formidable: limited mobile bandwidth, poor microphone quality, and the computational challenge of matching a tiny audio fingerprint against millions of songs.

Instead of seeking certainty before proceeding, Barton and his cofounders embraced wonder. "We didn't know if it would work," he admitted, "but we were driven by curiosity about what might be possible."

Their approach to uncertainty became their greatest strength. Unable to process audio recognition on phones (the necessary computing power took decades), they created an elegant work-around: Users would dial a number, hold their phone to the music for thirty seconds, then hang up. Shazam's servers would process the sample and send back the song information via text message.

This "wonder-based" approach led to innovations that overcame seemingly insurmountable technical barriers:

- **Audio Fingerprinting:** Rather than analyzing entire songs, they developed algorithms that created compact "fingerprints" of audio spectrogram peaks, making matching possible even with background noise.

- **Database Efficiency:** Instead of storing complete songs, they stored only these distinctive fingerprints, reducing database requirements by orders of magnitude.

- **Pattern Recognition:** They focused on identifying unique patterns within songs that could survive transmission through poor-quality phone microphones.

What's remarkable about Shazam's story goes beyond technological innovation to how Barton's team approached uncertainty itself. "The gap between what we knew was possible and what we dreamed might be possible was enormous," Barton explained. "We lived in that gap for years."

Facing a 0.01 percent chance of success according to industry experts, Barton persisted through eighteen investor rejections. The company launched in 2002 with a simple value proposition: "2580"—the number users dialed to identify songs. What began as an improbable idea eventually transformed how people interact with music, with over one billion downloads and an acquisition by Apple for $400 million in 2018.

Barton's advice for innovators facing uncertainty mirrors the Cone of Possibilities framework: "Don't wait for certainty—it will never come. Instead, develop hypotheses, test them rapidly, and let curiosity guide your exploration." The Shazam story demonstrates how working in wonder—embracing curiosity instead of demanding certainty—can transform seemingly impossible challenges into breakthrough innovations. By acknowledging what they didn't know but might discover, Barton's team created a category-defining product that changed how millions of people experience music.

PART TWO

DESIGN THE FUTURE

9
Strategy
Is Sacrifice

One Quantum Leap Forward, Sixty Steps Back

Lee's mood darkened as another wave of market alerts flooded his neural display.

"They're not just beating us on features anymore." Sarah's replacement, James, projected his analysis into the shared space. "Their quantum integration means they can process complex queries fifty times faster than our current architecture. We need to match this, maybe even surpass it."

The Gardens' ambient displays filled with proposals from various teams: quantum computing initiatives, AI acceleration projects, potential acquisitions. Each one promised to help Artemis catch up with Delta's capabilities. Each one required significant resources.

"If we move quickly," James continued, "we could have a comparable quantum system within six months. We'd need to redirect 40 percent of our engineering resources, but—"

"No," Lee interrupted, his voice quiet but firm.

The room fell silent. Through the smart glass, Seattle's tech corridor gleamed in the morning sun, each soaring building a testament to their industry's third chain of change: the comfort with adding more, doing more, acquiring more—always more.

"But, Lee," Maya from Operations said with mock horror, "are you suggesting we *don't* follow the 'throw everything at the wall and see what sticks' strategy that's worked so well for us before?"

Lee raised an eyebrow. "I know, shocking. Next, I'll suggest we actually listen to what our users want instead of what our competitors are doing."

"Blasphemy," Maya whispered, a smile tugging at the corner of her mouth.

Lee recognized the pattern. They'd spent years adding features, buying companies, expanding capabilities. It was comfortable, predictable. When in doubt, add more. When threatened, buy more. When challenged, build more.

"But, Lee," James interjected, radiating concern, "Delta's quantum announcement isn't just about technology. Our customers are already asking what our response will be. We need to show them we're not falling behind."

"What if falling behind on quantum computing is exactly what we need to do?" Lee replied.

Maya glared at Lee, then softened her gaze. "Look." Maya sighed, leaning back in her chair. "I'd sacrifice the entire third-floor meditation lounge before cutting any features, and that's saying something considering it's the only place I can escape the engineering team's debates about code architecture."

"Funny." Lee smiled. "I'd give up the office BaristaBot before I cut anything, and that's saying something considering what passes for coffee around here. Aren't we supposed to have good coffee here in Seattle?"

"Our coffee is that bad because Operations cut the budget three years ago," Maya shot back with a grin. "Some sacrifices have lasting consequences, you know."

Running in the Opposite Direction

Before anyone could protest further, Ava's voice cut through the tension.

"Does anyone remember when the world was clamoring to go electric?" she began. "Back in 2024, when every automotive company was racing to go all electric, Toyota made what seemed like a catastrophic decision."

"Aria, pull up Toyota's 2024 strategic decisions." The Gardens' displays shifted. "Toyota had spent decades building expertise in hybrid technology. Its Prius had revolutionized the industry in the early 2000s. In 2024, while Tesla's market cap soared and traditional automakers scrambled to announce all-electric lineups, Toyota doubled down on hybrids."

The visualizations showed market reactions, as Ava continued: "Wall Street predicted Toyota's doom. Analysts demanded they follow competitors into all-electric development. Instead, Toyota chose to optimize what they did best. They saw what others missed—that infrastructure and technology weren't ready for mass EV adoption. They chose to sacrifice the appearance of innovation for actual differentiation.

"They left their chips on the table where they'd played them. In 2025, Toyota announced a partnership with NVIDIA that transformed their approach to autonomous vehicles. "Instead of trying to beat Tesla and BYD at their own game, they created an entirely new one—combining their hybrid expertise with advanced AI to create unique value.

Why we work **determines *how* we collaborate.**

"And what does our world look like today, a decade later?" Ava asked, gesturing to the data streams showing current market share. "It's not dominated by EVs or hybrids alone. It's both. While other manufacturers scrambled to switch entirely to electric, Toyota's strategic sacrifice paid off. They lead in autonomous hybrid vehicles while Tesla's electric segment has been consumed by cheaper alternatives—Toyota picked a core offering to be the best in the world at. They let the market catch up to their vision instead of chasing someone else's."

Lee studied the market visualization. "They turned their constraint into a competitive advantage."

As the data continued to flow across the Gardens' smart surfaces, he noticed something else. "They won by deleting options, not adding them."

"Exactly." Ava nodded. "Strategy isn't just about what you pursue: It's about what you deliberately eliminate. This brings us to the fourth Innovation Principle." On the digital whiteboard, she wrote:

Mindset shift from adding more differentiation → **deleting for differentiation**

Innovation Principle 4: Strategy Is Sacrifice

Lee absorbed this insight and said, "Aria, show me our monthly feature usage data."

The air filled with a complex web of Artemis' offerings. The visualization was stunning in its clarity: of their hundreds of features, only 40 percent saw regular monthly use. The most engaged features weren't their processing-heavy functions but their human-interaction capabilities.

"We've been trapped in the chain of comfort," Lee realized aloud. "Not just comfort with the status quo but comfort with constant addition. Every threat, every challenge, every competition—we respond by adding more.

"Why we work determines how we collaborate," Lee said, his voice carrying a new conviction. "The depth of your connection determines the height of your collaboration. And somehow we've lost that depth along the way."

He moved to the digital whiteboard and began writing:

CHAIN OF CHANGE:
Comfort with Status Quo—Addition

- Adding features to match competitors
- Acquiring companies for capabilities
- Building more to solve problems
- Expanding scope to capture market

"Here's my proposal," Lee said. "We delete every feature that isn't used at least monthly by our users. Based on this data, that's 60 percent of our current offerings."

The room erupted.

"But we spent years building those features at Tech-Minds," James protested.

"And our users spent years not using them," Lee countered. "Look at the data. Our most valuable features aren't our fastest or most complex. They're the ones that enhance human-AI collaboration."

"But once we delete them—"

"You're thinking about it as a point of no return," Lee interrupted, a memory surfacing from his early days in product management. "Jeff Bezos had an interesting framework for decisions like this. He called them one-way and two-way doors."

Two-Way Door Decisions

The Gardens' displays shifted to illustrate the concept. "Two-way door decisions are reversible—like testing a new feature or changing a user interface. You can always walk back through the door if it doesn't work. But one-way door decisions," Lee continued, "are like moving to a new city or, in Amazon's case, acquiring Whole Foods. Once you walk through, there's no easy way back."

"And deleting 60 percent of our features is a one-way door," Maya observed.

"Actually, it's not." Lee smiled. "We're not deleting the code—we're deactivating features. If we're wrong, we can bring them back. And here's what Bezos understood: We often treat reversible decisions as irreversible ones, which leads to slow, overcautious movement when we should be experimenting and learning."

"Amazon used this framework to make faster decisions about everything from new products to entire business lines," Ava added. "They could move quickly on two-way door decisions while giving appropriate consideration to true one-way decisions."

Lee turned back to the usage data hovering around them. "Our real one-way door decision isn't about deleting features; it's about what we choose to become. Do we want to be another quantum AI company, or do we want to be the company that truly understands human-AI collaboration?"

James studied the data with fresh eyes. "Our users have already been telling us which door to walk through," he realized. "Look at the engagement patterns. They're choosing human-centered features over raw processing power every time."

James hesitated briefly before seeming to commit—and outlined a proposal on the whiteboard:

To Delete:

- 60 percent of underutilized features
- Quantum processing initiatives
- Noncore acquisitions
- Legacy system maintenance

To Focus On:

- Human-AI interaction
- Emotional intelligence algorithms
- Collaborative intelligence
- Accessibility features

"James, I'm glad you're getting it. This isn't just cost-cutting." Lee smiled. "This is strategic sacrifice. Every feature we maintain diverts resources from our core strength. Every capability we chase dilutes our focus."

Maya's avatar shifted forward. "The operational implications..."

"...will transform our entire infrastructure," Lee finished. "Imagine the efficiency gains from a simplified architecture. The resources we could redirect to true innovation."

Maya wasn't convinced. "You know what we call a simplified architecture in Operations? A unicorn. Mythical, beautiful, and about as real as our last five-year strategic plan. But I'm willing to suspend my disbelief for once if it means I can stop explaining to the board why our servers need therapy."

The depth of
your connection
**determines the
height of your
collaboration.**

Beyond Conventional

"Toyota's hybrid strategy wasn't just about technology," Ava added. "It was about understanding their unique value proposition. They sacrificed the race for pure electric vehicles so they could dominate the hybrid market they'd pioneered."

The Gardens' displays showed the potential impact: streamlined development paths, reduced technical debt, focused innovation pipelines. But more importantly, they showed something else: a clear differentiation from Delta's quantum-focused approach.

"Delta can win the processing race," Lee concluded. "Let them. We'll win by going beyond conventional, by understanding humans better than any other AI company in the world. That's not just strategy—that's differentiation through deletion."

Beyond the smart glass, Seattle's tech corridor hummed with the constant push for more. Inside Artemis, a different energy was building. The third chain of change, Comfort with the Status Quo, was beginning to break.

"This isn't about cutting features; it is about developing the Change Fluency to recognize when addition is creating clutter rather than value," Maya said, her operational concerns shifting to opportunities. "The maintenance savings alone..."

"... could fund our human-centered AI research for years," James finished, his skepticism giving way to possibility.

The Gardens' living walls bloomed with new patterns as the team began mapping features for deletion. In choosing what to eliminate, they were finally discovering what they could become.

Sometimes, Lee realized, the most innovative strategy isn't running faster in the same direction—it's having the courage to run in a different direction entirely. And sometimes, the key to standing out isn't adding more features but deleting everything that stands between you and your true differentiation.

Principle 4: Strategy Is Sacrifice

Your greatest differentiation comes not from what you
add but from what you have the courage to eliminate.

Key Takeaways & Considerations

How do we innovate when we're consumed by maintaining what we've already built?

Strategy isn't about doing more: It's about doing less, better. True differentiation comes not from adding capabilities but from making deliberate choices about what to eliminate.

Key Principles

Strategic Sacrifice: Strategic sacrifice demands the courage to eliminate good options in service of great ones. It recognizes that what you choose not to do defines your path as powerfully as what you pursue. Just as Toyota's focused hybrid strategy created sustainable advantage, deliberate sacrifice creates space for excellence in your chosen domain.

Disruption Is Deletion: Innovation often emerges not from addition but from thoughtful elimination. When we deliberately remove elements that don't serve our core purpose, we create clarity and focus that drive meaningful differentiation. By maintaining fewer, better offerings, we can create deeper impact and stronger positioning instead of trying to be everything to everyone.

Decision Framework: Understanding the difference between reversible and irreversible decisions enables bolder strategic choices. By using the two-way door concept, teams can move quickly on reversible decisions while giving appropriate consideration to true one-way choices. This framework helps maintain focus on core strengths rather than reactive competitive matching.

Warning Signs of Poor Strategy: When teams constantly add new initiatives without removing existing ones, they risk diluting their impact. The inability to say no to opportunities often masks a deeper inability to define what truly matters. Watch for the tendency to match every competitor's move or spread resources too thinly across multiple priorities. These patterns signal the need for more strategic sacrifice.

Put It into Practice: Strategic Sacrifice

The **Strategic Sacrifice** exercise helps functional leaders identify what to eliminate in order to strengthen their core impact. Like a sculptor removing excess stone to reveal the masterpiece within, you'll learn to cut away nonessential elements to unveil your team's true value proposition.

Get started at changefluency.com/bookresources or scan the QR code.

10
Leverage Your Limits

Running to Catch Up

The early morning mist clung to the surface of Lake Union as Lee completed his third lap. His running shoes pounded rhythmically against the lakeside path, each impact sending small jolts through his body that reminded him of his newfound vulnerability. The doctor had suggested "moderate exercise" after his diagnosis—a term Lee had interpreted as permission to continue his morning runs.

He paused at the lake's eastern shore, watching as a float plane descended toward the water, pushing out gentle ripples that distorted the reflection of Seattle's skyline. His neural display pinged, flashing another alert about Delta's quantum breakthrough. Even here, in what should have been his moment of peace, the professional crisis shadowed him.

"CRITICAL: Delta Tech builds on quantum AI breakthrough; new partnership agreement announcement with the top ten Fortune 500 companies. Artemis stock predicted to drop 18 percent at market open."

"How do they keep doing this?" A direct message from James, his lead architect, popped up in Lee's chat. "It's like they're not even playing by the same rules."

"Maybe we don't need to either," Lee mused, his mind roaming to find the signal in the noise. "We're looking at this all wrong."

Unlike the paralyzing panic of months ago, Lee felt something different stirring—a clarity born from crisis. Stopping by a park bench, he threw a foot on it to stretch a little as he pulled up Artemis' metrics, looking not at what they lacked compared to Delta but at what made them unique.

"I thought I might find you here," Ava's voice cut through his thoughts. She stood a few yards away, out of place in her casual clothes among the morning joggers in their performance gear.

Lee raised an eyebrow. "How did you know?"

"Maya mentioned you run here most mornings. Said it helps you think." Ava gestured toward the path. "Mind if I walk the last lap with you?"

They fell into step together, Lee slowing his pace as Ava matched his rhythm.

"Beautiful out here," she observed, looking across the water where the sun was starting to burn through the mist. "I can see why you come."

"Been running this loop since my college days," Lee admitted. "Three miles exactly. Used to time myself religiously—always trying to beat my personal best." He gave a rueful laugh. "Now, I'm just grateful to complete it."

"The tumor?" Ava asked directly, in her characteristic way.

Lee nodded. "Doctor says it's not a contraindication, but I've been thinking about constraints a lot lately. How our limitations shape us." He gestured toward his neural display where Delta's announcement still pulsed. "Both personally and professionally."

"And what have you concluded?" Ava asked as they rounded the northern edge of the lake, the Space Needle coming into view.

"I'm starting to wonder if we've been looking at this all wrong," Lee said, his breath forming small clouds in the cool morning air. "We've been seeing our constraints as weaknesses: my health, our processing limitations compared to Delta. But what if they're actually pointing us toward our greatest opportunities?"

Ava raised an eyebrow, appearing more evaluative. "Oh? Tell me more."

"Delta's quantum processing is impressive. But look at our user engagement patterns." He projected the data into the space between them. "Our 'slower' processing actually creates more meaningful interactions. Users spend 42 percent more time in collaborative sessions. Team cohesion scores are up 31 percent. We've been seeing our technical limitations as weaknesses, but what if... "

"... they're actually our strength?" Ava finished, a smile playing at her lips. "You're starting to see the patterns."

"I had a good teacher," Lee replied, then frowned. "But there's something else here I can't quite grasp. We're missing a bigger principle about limitations themselves."

Ava's eyes sparkled with that familiar mix of challenge and approval. "What's the most valuable consumer packaged retail brand in the world?"

The question seemed so disconnected from their crisis that Lee almost ignored it. "Procter & Gamble?" he guessed, distracted by another alert about Delta's quantum breakthrough.

"Back in the early 2020s, I was shocked to learn that it was Costco's Kirkland Signature."

"Wait, Costco?" Lee glanced at Ava curiously; she had his attention.

The Surprising Truth Behind Costco

"Yup. That notion led me down the deepest of rabbit holes. I couldn't help but ask myself, 'Why? What drives their innovation? How do they disrupt?' You see, intuitively I knew Costco was a mammoth, but the biggest?" Ava shook her head in disbelief, as if still shocked.

She continued, "Think about the biggest retailers we frequent—and what makes them special.

"Walmart—my first job was at Walmart; I used to unload trucks in shipping and receiving. And I remember, plastered on all the walls and throughout the aisles, was everything Walmart stood for—the lowest everyday *price*.

"And then I thought about Amazon. Amazon is all about *convenience*, not price. I moved to a new house last month, and whenever I needed something, I just added it to my Prime delivery for the next day. I knew I was paying more, but I also didn't have to leave my house.

"But Costco? It's playing an entirely different ball-game when it comes to disruption. What's unique about how Costco has disrupted the entire retail industry is not by what it chooses to do; what is unique is what Costco chooses not to do. It's how Costco leverages its limits.

"And this got me thinking, how do we leverage our limits to become differentiated in *our* marketplace?"

Ava launched into the origin story of Costco. "In the 1950s, a Jewish lawyer from the Bronx, Solomon Price, moves to San Diego. Back then, San Diego was nothing like the city it is today. At the time, it had a small population of 150,000 people and was modestly growing.

"Sol has a flourishing legal practice there. One of his clients is Four Star Jewelry. As he partners with them, he learns that 70 percent of all their wholesale business comes from one customer, a group called FEDCO.

"FEDCO has eight hundred federal workers, mostly postal workers. They're a nonprofit collective that, after World War II, came together to pool their purchasing power to buy large amounts of goods for lower prices. FEDCO's business model is that they charge a small membership fee, and in exchange, their members can get their everyday household items for cheaper than the other big box retailers.

"Sol sees the opportunity. He launches FedMart, which eventually becomes Price Club, then Costco."

Ava, who had been getting increasingly excited, takes a breath and pauses before continuing.

"What's remarkable to me is how Sol makes key decisions on the limits he would like to place on FedMart. By digging deep into the constraints that most big retailers face, Sol was able to reimagine retail as we know it. In fact, his legacy is his brand. He was known as the king of retail, praised by Sam Walton and so many others, and shaped the pathway for Kmart, Walmart, Target, you name it, to deliver retail as we know it today. At least before e-commerce took over." Ava laughed.

"It's an important shift in mindset," she said, "and the fifth Innovation Principle":

Mindset shift from limits as obstacles   →   **limits as catalysts**

Innovation Principle 5: Leverage Your Limits

"Which leads us to this question: How does Costco define its limits?

"The first way is they limit their profits. You see, most retail companies look for the most margins, right? They're asking, 'How much can we possibly earn from everything that we're selling?' No surprise there. Just another day in our capitalist world.

"But what's different about Costco is that they limit their profit margins to 14, maximum 15 percent. They then pass on the rest of the profit to their customers as savings.

"The second thing they limit is their warehouse inventory. Think about it. Costco is literally the only warehouse I buy anything from. By limiting how their space is set up, Costco employees don't unload anything off pallets. In fact, it's basically self-service. You want something? You go ahead and get it yourself, straight off the pallet."

Ava grabbed a stick and wrote down the number 260,000 in the sand. She considered something, then double-underlined her scribble.

This is so good, Lee said to himself as he nodded along.

"Costco also limits the amount of inventory they carry. You see, most retailers have about 260,000 different, unique items in any store. But Costco only sells three to four thousand items.

"They have the most limited inventory ever, but what they choose are the most frequently purchased items. What's remarkable is that by doing this, they're able to focus on the small number of goods that produce the most purchases as a result."

Disruption Is Discipline

Ava's eyes sparked with intensity. "How do you package lightning in a bottle?" she asked. "Most people think disruption happens through random flashes of genius. But what Costco shows us is that true disruption requires rigorous discipline. Inspiration is fleeting, striking like lightning, so make the most of it when it comes. But transforming an industry? That takes consistent, deliberate practice."

Lee nodded, seeing the connection. "Disruption isn't the opposite of discipline; it's the result of it."

"Exactly." Ava smiled. "The most innovative companies aren't chaotic. They've just chosen different rules to follow than everyone else."

"Hmm, here at Artemis, we do a *lot* of things," Lee said. "As Delta has taken over our position as the market leader in work collaboration platforms, this reminds me about how we're starting to reduce the number of services and tools we provide to focus on the ones that matter most."

Seeing the wheels turning in Lee's mind, Ava paused to hold space.

Lee asked himself, *How* do *we leverage our limits and focus on doing less but better?*

"Last but not least, Costco limits how much marketing they focus on. They don't really market their services or products that much. They don't really advertise."

"Right," said Lee, "they have their Costco magazine that you get once a month in the mail."

"And what's remarkable about Costco is that since the 1970s, they've leaned into providing so much value that their customers rave about them. And now, sixty years later, because their customers love them so much, they're

True disruption
requires rigorous discipline.

able to leverage TikTok, Instagram, and every other social media platform. Costco doesn't have to focus much of their resources there. In fact, most of their referrals to this day continue to be driven by word-of-mouth. Which we all know is way more powerful than advertising. Not to mention, free."

Half processing Ava's observation, half jumping into solution, Lee blurted, "Thinking about Delta's quantum announcement, it isn't just about technology—it's about market perception. Those Fortune 500 partnerships? They're betting on processing power over human connection.

"What if we make an equally bold bet but in the opposite direction?" Lee stopped in his tracks on the gravel pathway. "What if we stopped apologizing for our constraints and started highlighting them? 'Yes, we process slower—because we prioritize understanding over speed. Yes, we have fewer features—because we value depth over breadth.'"

"Dangerous strategy," Ava challenged. "The board's already nervous about our market position."

"More dangerous to chase Delta's game, which feels like a terribly steep uphill battle," Lee countered. "Costco didn't try to match Walmart's selection or Amazon's convenience. They turned their limitations into their brand. We need to do the same."

Disruption Is a Game of Constraints

"Love where you're going with this, Lee," Ava encouraged him. "Disruption is a game of constraints. Trade-offs. Limitations.

"Most people think that our limits hold us back," she added, "but really, it's our limits that set us free."

Damn, that's good. Lee chuckled to himself. *I should put that on a coffee mug.*

"You're mentally designing merchandise with my quotes again, aren't you?" Ava smirked, eyebrow raised. "Just remember, I get royalties on anything over a thousand units."

They were reaching the final stretch of the lake path, as Ava observed, "Costco didn't just accept their constraints; they weaponized them. Limited selection became curated excellence. Minimal marketing became word-of-mouth power. Their limitations created their competitive advantage. You see, we drive disruption not by what we do but by what we choose *not* to do."

Lee stopped walking and popped open his water bottle to take a quick swig. "So, for Artemis, our limitation of focusing on human-centered AI rather than pure processing power..."

"... could be exactly what sets us apart," Ava finished. "Delta can win the quantum race. Let them. Remember that we'll win by understanding humans better than any other AI company in the world.

"That's what Change Fluency truly means," Ava added. "Being fluent in a new language doesn't mean that you have mastered every word in the dictionary, but instead that you are able to express yourself sufficiently *despite* your vocabulary limits."

As they approached the entrance to Artemis, Lee signaled that he was going to head to the changerooms. Passing by, Lee could see his team gathering for the morning standup, their AR displays already active with the day's challenges.

"You know what's ironic?" Lee touched the small scar from his recent surgery. "My tumor felt like the ultimate constraint: this tiny thing limiting everything. But it taught me to see differently. It made me focus on what matters most: human connection, authentic care, real impact."

Ava nodded. "The question isn't 'How do we remove our constraints?' It's 'How do we transform them into advantages?' Sarah's departure forced us to develop new capabilities we wouldn't have discovered otherwise. Speaking of which..." She gestured to Lee's neural display. "Ready to show your team how to play the constraint game?"

Lee smiled, thinking of Costco's journey from limited selection to market dominance. "First, we need to identify our sandbox—map out our constraints clearly. Only then can we start reimagining the boundaries."

"You've come a long way from the man who wanted to match Delta feature for feature," Ava observed.

"I'm learning! Time to make our limits work for us," he said excitedly, switching direction to head straight to the team gathering. "After all, if Costco could turn constraints into billions, imagine what Artemis could do with theirs.

"By the way, you know what's funny about working with TechMinds?" Lee said. "They hold 'silent meetings' where everyone types simultaneously in a shared document. First time I joined, I kept talking for ten minutes before realizing no one was listening. Our teams communicate so differently, it makes the United Nations look like a high-school debate club."

Lee glanced at Ava. "You know, I never thanked you."

"For what?"

"For not firing me that first day like Elena threatened," Lee said with a half smile. "Given how things have played out, I'm thinking I owe you one."

Ava waved dismissively. "Elena's too quick to burn bridges when she's scared. I've always found it more interesting to see what people build under pressure. You've proven me right." She paused. "Ready to help me plan how to bring five thousand employees along on this journey?"

Before Lee could reply, Ava continued, "Actually, I think it's time you did this one on your own. For all my talk about the importance of boundaries and personal renewal..."

She paused, her fingers tapping rhythmically against her side.

"I haven't been great at practicing what I preach. Did you know I haven't taken more than a week off in three years? Even during those so-called vacations, I was constantly checking in."

Lee noticed something different in her demeanor—a subtle vulnerability he rarely saw in the woman who seemed to have all the answers. "What are you saying?"

"I'm taking a sabbatical," Ava replied, her voice gaining certainty with the words. "Twelve months, starting next month. Argentina first, then wherever the journey takes me."

The news hit Lee with unexpected force. "Twelve months? But we're just starting to gain traction against Delta." He paused, still trying to grasp the news. "What does Elena think about this?"

"She's not thrilled," Ava admitted. "But I reminded her that we've been preaching authenticity and purpose to the whole organization. If I can't honor my own need for renewal, what kind of example am I setting?"

As the morning sun extended across the Gardens, Lee realized that this, too, was part of the journey—learning not just to champion change but to embrace it when it arrived unexpectedly in his own life.

"So," he said finally, "how do we make the most of the time we have left?"

Principle 5: Leverage Your Limits

Your constraints aren't holding you back; they're pointing
toward your unique competitive advantage.

Key Takeaways & Considerations

How do we create meaningful differentiation when everyone has access to the same tools and technology?

True differentiation often comes not from removing
constraints but from transforming them into competitive
advantages. Organizations that thrive don't just work within
their limits; they leverage them to create unique value.

Key Principles

Constraints as Strategy: In the journey of transformation,
limitations aren't obstacles to overcome but boundaries that
define uniqueness. The most innovative solutions often
emerge from embracing and working within constraints
rather than from unlimited resources. Just as Costco turned
its limited inventory into a cornerstone of its success,
restrictions can become the catalyst for creative problem-solving that sets an organization apart.

Finding Power in Parameters: When organizations
reframe their relationship with constraints, they discover
unexpected sources of competitive advantage. Rather than
seeing limitations as weaknesses to overcome, successful
organizations study their constraints deeply to understand
how they might create unique value. Like Costco's membership model, which turned limited access into premium
value, constraints can become defining features that attract
rather than repel customers.

Scaling Through Limits: True growth doesn't require
removing all limitations; instead, it demands learning to
thrive within them. The right constraints can enable faster
scaling by creating clear operating principles that guide
decision-making and resource allocation. Like Costco's

limited products enabling better supplier relationships and operational efficiency, well-defined constraints can strengthen core capabilities while creating sustainable competitive advantages.

Put It into Practice: Transform Your Constraints

Instead of seeing limitations as obstacles, this exercise helps functional leaders transform constraints into strategic advantages. Like a chef turning a small kitchen into a specialized dining experience, let's make your limitations work for you.

Transform Your Constraints into an advantage at changefluency.com/bookresources or scan the QR code.

Fuel or Fumes

Signals That Your Team Is Burning Bright— or Burning Out

What's the secret to bringing teams along during transformation without burning them out?

In transformation efforts, the line between energized momentum and exhausted resignation can be surprisingly thin. Use these indicators to determine whether your team is running on fuel or fumes.

Running on Fuel

What you'll hear:

- "I'm excited about where this is taking us."
- "I can see how much progress we're making."
- "It feels like we're really jamming as a team."
- "I had an idea that could make this even better."
- "Let me show you what I've been working on."

What you'll observe: You'll notice spontaneous collaboration as team members cross traditional boundaries to work together. Problems are consistently framed as challenges to overcome rather than complaints to air. Team members actively build on each other's ideas, creating a multiplying effect. Healthy debate remains focused on improving outcomes, not dwelling on obstacles. Perhaps most tellingly, energy levels actually increase during group sessions, with people leaving more energized than when they arrived.

Running on Fumes

What you'll hear:

- "Things are going so, so well!" (with an eye roll)
- "Whatever you think is best." (with a disengaged tone)
- "It doesn't really matter—we'll get pointed in a different direction in six months anyway."
- "What's the point?"
- "I'm just here so I don't get fired."

What you'll observe: Increased sarcasm and cynical humor permeate conversations, often masking deeper frustrations. Participation in meetings and discussions steadily declines, with cameras off and minimal engagement. Team members focus on compliance rather than contribution, doing exactly what's asked and nothing more. Idea sharing and innovation submissions drop dramatically as people stop investing discretionary effort. Most visibly, energy noticeably depletes during team gatherings, with people checking out mentally or appearing visibly drained afterward.

The Tipping Point

Most concerning is when teams shift from positive skepticism ("I have concerns, but I'm willing to engage") to resigned compliance ("I'll do it because I have to"). This transition often happens gradually, making it difficult to detect until engagement metrics have already plummeted.

Teams don't typically move from fuel to fumes because the work is hard—they shift when the work feels meaningless. The antidote isn't reducing challenge but reconnecting effort to purpose.

11
Paint a Bigger Canvas

Lemongrass and Chili Oil

The aroma of lemongrass and chili oil wafted through Lee's kitchen as guests mingled at his dinner party. His neural display was mercifully quiet—he'd promised Teresa he'd be present tonight—but thoughts of Artemis' challenges lingered. They'd made progress in leveraging their constraints, focusing on human connection over pure processing power, but the board still wanted more. Growth. Scale. Impact.

"You have to try this," Teresa insisted, pulling him toward a woman standing by the kitchen island. "Mai's chili oil is incredible. She's the woman I told you about, the one who quit her engineering job to start her own business."

Mai smiled warmly, offering a spoonful of crimson oil that shimmered in the kitchen's ambient lighting. "Family recipe, but with a twist. My *bà nội*, my grandmother, would probably be scandalized by what I've done with it."

Lee tasted it, his eyes widening at the complex layers of flavor. "This is amazing. You make this yourself?"

Mai nodded. "Started in my kitchen two years ago. Now, we're in thirty-seven states and expanding to Canada next month. Not bad for a side project that started because I missed my grandmother's cooking."

"Thirty-seven states? How did you ... "

"... scale?" Mai finished. "Actually, it's funny you should ask. I was struggling with marketing, trying to compete with these massive condiment companies. Then I discovered the epic story behind Canva and its founder Melanie Perkins."

Lee's product leader instincts kicked in. "The design platform?"

"More than that." Mai pulled out her phone, showing a series of stunning product shots, recipe cards, and social media posts. "You know, before Canva, Adobe had created the most powerful design tools in the world. But Melanie saw something different: She saw all the people who weren't being served. The teachers, small-business owners, students... billions of people who needed to create visual content but lacked the technical skills or resources. That meant she had a total addressable market, or TAM, whose needs weren't being met."

She swiped through her gallery. "Professional graphic design used to mean expensive software, complicated tools. Adobe was the gold standard, but it was like trying to use a rocket ship when I just needed a bicycle. Canva didn't try to build a better Photoshop; it built something different entirely."

The parallels suddenly clicked for Lee. "They expanded the market from thousands of professional designers to millions of everyday creators."

"Right," Mai said, smiling. "And they did it thoughtfully, staying true to their core mission of making design accessible. Started with basic social media tools, then added templates for specific industries, moved into enterprise collaboration, video and website design, brand management... Each step expanded their reach while staying true to their purpose."

Mai drizzled her chili oil over some appetizers. "You know what's funny? When I started, I thought the chili oil market was crowded, saturated. But what has worked wonders for me is finding my niche where people were drawn to me personally. What I was really selling was connection. A simple bowl of *bún bò huế* complemented with my chili oil led to our culture, to our memories, to our family traditions. Sometimes your real opportunity isn't in the product itself but in what it enables for people."

Her words hit home. Artemis wasn't just building faster AI—they were building more understanding AI. And in a world racing toward automation, maybe that understanding was exactly what people needed most.

"Admittedly, I don't follow much news in the business world, so I'm surprised that I've heard about your company, but I guess there's a lot going on with your competitors," Mai said, tilting her head. "You know what's ironic though? Your company, Artemis, is named after the goddess of the hunt, and now you're realizing you don't need to hunt down Delta after all."

Lee raised his eyebrows.

"I guess I learned something in my Intro to Greek Mythology class in university after all." Mai's eyes twinkled.

Lee snorted. "So, we've been chasing our tail this whole time? Figures. Maybe we should've named ourselves after the god of naps instead."

"Hypnos Tech does have a certain ring to it." Mai laughed, as Lee poured them a gin and tonic.

Start with the Base

Later that evening, after most guests had left, Lee found himself back in the kitchen with Mai. She was carefully packaging her remaining chili oil while he cleaned dishes, their conversation turning deeper.

"The fascinating thing about Canva's growth," Mai said, "was how methodical it was. Like a good recipe, they got the base right first."

She pulled up pictures of her bottles of chili oil, each one representing a different stage of her business. "When I started, I wanted to do everything: different flavors, different sizes, different markets. But I learned from studying Canva's journey. They started with a single, clear focus: making design accessible. Everything else built from there."

"Hmm." Lee dried his hands, then pulled up his neural display, projecting it so Mai could see. "Show me Canva's growth trajectory."

The data hovered between them, glowing softly in the dim kitchen:

- basic design tools for social media
- templates for specific industries
- enterprise collaboration features
- video and website design
- brand management and workflow tools

"Each expansion wasn't about adding features," Mai observed. "It was about serving more people who needed accessible design tools. They didn't dilute their focus; they applied it to new problems and markets."

Lee thought about the recent experiments from Jen's team at TechMinds. "We've been seeing something similar with our emotional AI. It started as a way to improve business communication, but people are finding new uses we never imagined."

"Like what?"

"A teacher in Buenos Aires uses it to notice when students are struggling but might be too shy to speak up. A doctor in Singapore says it helps maintain the human element in virtual consultations. An elder care facility is testing it to provide better emotional support for residents."

Mai's eyes lit up. "So, like Canva, your technology could serve entirely new markets that value understanding over speed."

"Exactly. We've been so focused on competing with Delta's quantum processing—"

"When you could be expanding into markets where processing speed isn't even the main concern," Mai finished. "You know, in cooking, there's a saying: 'When the pie isn't going to feed everyone, don't fight for scraps—bake a bigger pie.'"

The next morning, Lee pinged Ava: "My dinner party sparked some interesting ideas about market expansion. Gardens, 9 a.m.?"

When Ava arrived, Lee was sitting on a picnic table, a box of Mai's chili oil on the table. "I have something for you." He pushed it toward her as an offering. "Quite the product story—but that's for another time."

As Ava picked up the chili oil to examine her gift, Lee moved to the whiteboard, writing:

Mindset shift from competing in markets → **creating new markets**

Innovation Principle 6: Paint a Bigger Canvas

"I met this entrepreneur last night: Mai. She said something that stuck with me," Lee said. "When the pie gets too small to feed everyone, don't fight for scraps—bake a bigger pie. I keep thinking that it's really hard to differentiate from Delta, especially given how hard it is for us to match their quantum processing. But what if that limitation is actually pointing us toward our biggest opportunities?"

"Derivative products dilute the market, while differentiated products create new ones." Ava lit up, seeing where Lee was going. "Using our human-centered approach to serve markets that care more about understanding than speed. Look at you teaching me something new!"

Lee gestured to the Gardens' displays, bringing up potential market expansions:

- **Health Care:** Emotional support for patients, enhanced doctor-patient communication, mental health monitoring

- **Education:** Student engagement tracking, personalized learning adaptation, early intervention signals

- **Elder Care:** Emotional companion AI, family connection enhancement, care provider support

"Each one," Lee realized, "values our core strength in human understanding over pure processing power. We're not just trying to get a bigger piece of the enterprise collaboration pie ... "

"... we're baking entirely new pies," Ava finished with a smile.

Derivative products dilute the market; **differentiated products create new ones.**

Principle 6: Paint a Bigger Canvas

Instead of fighting for a bigger slice of the
existing pie, add something new to the pie—
or bake an entirely new pie.

Key Takeaways & Considerations

Expanding the TAM (total addressable market) is about growing the market instead of competing for a small slice of it. When things feel crowded, look for new customer segments, untapped opportunities, or fresh ways to create demand. Instead of fighting over scraps, make the pie bigger for everyone—or bake a new pie.

For leaders driving organizational transformation—whether you're in HR, finance, engineering, or other functions—expanding the TAM means shifting from a mindset of resource competition to one of value creation. Instead of fighting for limited budget, headcount, or influence, identify new ways to contribute to the organization's success.

This could mean redefining processes to unlock efficiencies, expanding talent pipelines to bring in fresh perspectives, or using data to uncover new strategic opportunities. By thinking beyond existing constraints, we can help grow the impact of our function and create more opportunities for the entire organization.

Key Principles

Expand Your Impact Zone: There are many ways leaders can grow the pie. Instead of competing for limited talent, HR leaders could create new talent pools through innovative development programs, unconventional hiring paths, or cross-functional skill-building initiatives. Rather than just allocating existing resources, finance leaders could identify new value creation opportunities through data analytics, process optimization, or innovative funding models. Engineering leaders could move beyond feature competition to create new technical capabilities that open unexplored possibilities for the organization. Operations leaders could move beyond optimizing existing processes by reimagining them. You'll start to transform constraints into opportunities.

Growth Through Value Creation: Shift from resource competition to opportunity expansion. Look for unmet needs within your sphere of influence. Transform limitations into catalysts for innovation.

From Function to Future: Redefine your role's contribution to organizational success. Identify unexplored areas where your expertise could add value. Create new opportunities rather than competing for existing ones.

Put It into Practice: Differentiation DNA Map

Like a chef discovering that their unique cooking style could create an entirely new cuisine category, the **Differentiation DNA Map** helps you identify your distinctive qualities and how they could create new value. Rather than just listing strengths, you'll uncover what truly makes you different and how that difference could matter to new audiences.

Get your PDF at changefluency.com/ bookresources or scan the QR code.

PART THREE

DIFFERENTIATE FROM THE STANDARD

12
Make Your Mission Personal

Sick of All the Change

The holographic dashboard pulsed with warning indicators as Lee reviewed the impact of what his team had started calling "perpetual transformation syndrome":

Change Initiatives (Last Six Months):

- Major reorganization: 3
- New technology platforms: 4
- Strategic pivots: 5

Team Impact:

- 68 percent report severe change fatigue.
- Monthly innovation submissions dropped from forty-seven to eight.
- Six senior engineers resigned citing "initiative exhaustion."

The ambient intelligence system had even started auto-generating burnout alerts based on team biometrics and communication patterns. "Warning: Collective cortisol levels 57 percent above baseline. Recommended action: Strategic pause."

Lee expanded the innovation submissions metric, trying to understand the dramatic drop. The Gardens' smart glass filled with historical data: Just six months ago, they'd averaged nearly fifty new ideas per month. Now, they were barely hitting eight.

"It's not that we don't have ideas," James said, materializing in his AR field as he joined from the development floor. His avatar's subtle blue glow marked him as joining remotely, but the frustration in his voice came through clearly. "It's that they're not being captured. Feedback from management has been to submit the form, but that's one extra step that nobody has time for—especially given our day-to-day tasks."

Lee sat with that for a moment, watching the innovation submission trends scroll past. "That's friction," he said, more to himself than James. "What should we do?" he wondered aloud.

James's avatar leaned forward, his expression brightening. "What if we integrated our AI avatar into that workflow? Someone could make an audible comment and add it to the pipeline?"

No Time for Innovation

The suggestion hung in the air between them, a simple solution to what they'd been treating as a complex problem. But Lee found himself stuck on something Sarah had said before she left: "Nobody has time." Making submissions easier would help, but it was also about why people no longer felt they could make time for innovation.

As Lee strolled through Artemis HQ, he could see his team at their workstations, neural interfaces glowing as they tackled their daily tasks. But what struck Lee most wasn't in the data. It was in the dead-eyed stares during standups, the way his once-passionate team now responded to every proposal with "Whatever you think is best." The same people who used to argue for hours about the ethical implications of AI architecture now sat silent in design reviews.

Lee noticed the subtle but telltale signs of the Apathy chain tightening: Team members who once leapt to volunteer now averted their eyes during brainstorms, conversations that once spilled over meeting times now ended fifteen minutes early.

They weren't just tired; they were emotionally disconnected from work that had once given them purpose.

"To advance human potential through adaptive intelligence," read Artemis' mission statement, floating in augmented reality above their collaboration space. The words seemed to mock the reality below, where his team's own adaptive potential was drowning in change fatigue.

"Yesterday, I heard Rachel from TechMinds say they were 'parking' an idea," James commented randomly with a grin. "Our engineers created an actual digital parking lot in the metaverse where their rejected ideas are stored as little cars. It's adorable and bizarre all at once. Maybe they're onto something?"

Lee was just about to respond when the Gardens' biometric lighting system shifted subtly as Ava entered, automatically adjusting to optimize for focused conversation. Around them, the living walls of self-organizing

Stats drive scores,
but stories stir souls.

plants—an experiment in ambient computing—rearranged their patterns in response to the changing light. She gestured at the warning indicators hovering in the air between them.

"Ah, you've discovered our fifth chain," she said, settling into her usual spot. "*Apathy*."

What Was Our Mission Statement Again?

"More like our fifth horseman of the apocalypse," Lee said with a sigh. "I've tried everything: new project structures, clearer goals, even increased autonomy. Nothing's working."

"Because you're treating the symptoms," Ava replied, "not the source."

She gestured to the displays, then hesitated. "Actually, I've been seeing the same thing with my team. Remember that big speech I gave about Change Fluency? The cowboys one?"

Lee nodded.

"Two days later, I overheard someone say, 'Another week, another transformation initiative.'" Ava's shoulders slumped slightly. "Even I'm not immune to creating change fatigue."

Lee was surprised by her admission. "What did you do?"

"I asked myself a question I should have asked sooner," Ava said, leaning forward. "When was the last time I asked my team why they came to Artemis in the first place?"

Lee started to respond, then stopped. He couldn't remember the last time he'd thought about his own why, let alone asked others about theirs.

"Here's what we know about transformation," Ava continued. "Change isn't solely about new structures or strategies. It's about meaning. When people lose their connection to meaning, apathy fills the void."

She pulled up a recent employee survey. "Look at this response: 'Another reorg, another reshuffling of deck chairs. Wake me when we remember why we're here.'

"Stats drive scores, but stories stir souls," Ava said quietly, her eyes meeting Lee's. "What's your forgotten story? We all have one. That's why you joined in the first place; it's your captivation with the organization. It's your personal attachment to the mission. It's the key to leading with heart."

"But we have a mission statement," Lee protested. "To advance human potential through adaptive intelligence."

Ava rolled her eyes dramatically. "Oh yes, and I'm sure your team recites it every morning while doing synchronized yoga poses."

"We tried that," Lee deadpanned. "Turns out 'adaptive intelligence' is really hard to say in downward dog position."

They shared a quick laugh, breaking the tension that had built up around the metrics.

"A mission statement could just be words on a wall. A mission statement isn't the same as a mission that's personal." Ava's eyes lit up with that familiar mix of challenge and possibility. "Want to understand the difference? Look at these."

She displayed a series of company missions:

- "Spread ideas." —TED

- "Entertain the world." —Netflix

- "Bring inspiration and innovation to every athlete in the world. (*If you have a body, you are an athlete.)" —Nike

- "We're in business to save our home planet." —Patagonia

"What makes these powerful isn't their poetry—it's their personal resonance. They connect organizational purpose to individual meaning. Did you know that 92 percent of Gen Z employees said purpose is critical to their job satisfaction? Not salary, not perks, not even technology. *Purpose.*"

The Power of Purpose

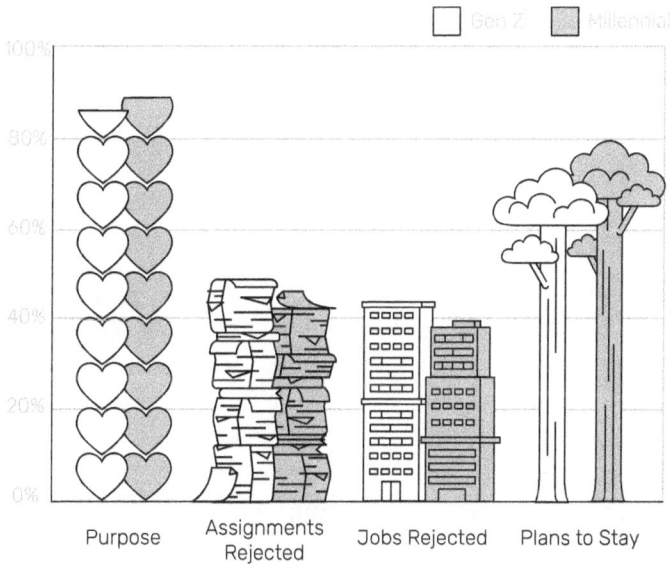

Deloitte's 2024 Gen Z and Millennial Survey reveals that 86 percent of Gen Zs and 89 percent of millennials consider having a sense of purpose in their work essential to job satisfaction and well-being. This emphasis on purpose is reflected in their career choices, with half of Gen Zs and

43 percent of millennials having rejected assignments that didn't align with their personal ethics, while 44 percent of Gen Zs and 40 percent of millennials have turned down potential employers for the same reason.

Both generations believe businesses have significant influence over societal challenges like environmental sustainability, ethical use of technology, and social equality, but less than half perceive that businesses are currently having a positive impact on society, indicating a gap between potential and performance.

When employers successfully align with employee values and respond positively to feedback, employee loyalty significantly increases, with 74 percent of Gen Zs and 79 percent of millennials planning to stay more than five years at organizations that demonstrate purpose alignment.

Want to break the chain of Apathy? Start with mission.

Lee thought about his daughter Grace's science fair project, that neural network that only worked "60 percent of the time," and the pride in his daughter's voice when she talked about AI helping people. When was the last time Lee had felt that kind of connection to his work?

"This brings us to our next mindset shifts," Ava said, standing to write on the whiteboard:

Mindset shift from mission as statement	→	**mission as story**
Mindset shift from purpose prescribed	→	**purpose cocreated**
Mindset shift from values displayed	→	**values lived**

When people lose their personal connection to purpose, **change becomes just another corporate exercise.**

Innovation Principle 7:
Make Your Mission Personal

"The greatest enemy of transformation isn't resistance—it's apathy," said Ava. "When people lose their personal connection to purpose, change becomes just another corporate exercise. But when they reconnect with their why, when they rediscover their personal stake in the mission, transformation becomes a way to better serve that purpose. It's impossible to push for transformation before you've anchored your teams in the familiar."

Lee looked again at his team's metrics, seeing them differently now. "We're not just fighting apathy, are we? We're fighting disengagement."

"Exactly. And you can't mandate meaning. You have to create space for people to find it themselves."

Lee nodded. "So, developing Change Fluency is about more than learning new processes or strategies..."

"... it's about becoming fluent in what matters to people," Ava finished. "It's not just knowing how to navigate transformation, but understanding why it matters on a personal level."

The Real Reason

The next morning, Lee stood in front of his team, acutely aware of the tension in the room. Instead of his planned reorganization update, he closed his laptop and moved from behind the podium.

"Ten years ago, my father gave me his old Microsoft developer badge," he began, perching on the edge of the conference table. "He'd kept it all those years after leaving Singapore for Seattle, chasing a dream of being part of the tech revolution. That badge represented everything he'd sacrificed for our family's future."

The atmosphere in the room shifted, subtle but noticeable. Even the most disengaged employees looked up from their devices.

"But that's not why I joined Artemis," Lee continued. "I joined because during my interview, I saw two engineers arguing passionately about whether their code would help a child with autism communicate better with their parents. They weren't discussing stock options or market share— they were fighting about impact. Real human impact.

"Aria, display our user impact stories." Lee nodded his head toward the room's immersive display.

"Your neural interface helped my daughter with cerebral palsy communicate for the first time. She told us she loves pizza."

"The adaptive AI made it possible for my father with dementia to keep his independence. It remembers for him what he's starting to forget."

"Your collaboration tools let me work remotely through my son's cancer treatment. I could be there for every appointment while still providing for my family."

"These aren't just testimonials—they're reminders of what our mission, 'advancing human potential,' really means. Every story represents someone whose life has been transformed by our work, your work—and yet somehow these impacts have gotten lost in the endless cycle of reorganizations and initiatives.

"Let's try something different," Lee said, gesturing to the mission floating above them: "To advance human potential through adaptive intelligence."

He thought about what Ava had taught him about Change Fluency: Driving change required a personal resonance with their mission.

When mission becomes personal, **change becomes purposeful.**

"What do these words mean to you? Not what you think they're supposed to mean, but how they connect to your own story."

He shared his own connection first. "For me, 'advancing human potential' isn't abstract. I see how productivity is enhanced and capacity is unlocked for millions of people as they lean into our platform. I see how I have time for walks in nature and board game nights because our AI agents are working for us. I see how my daughter Grace falls into a state of flow every time she tackles a new science fair project. Technology truly empowers the next generation."

The room was quiet, but it was a different kind of quiet—contemplative rather than apathetic.

"Take two minutes," Lee continued. "Write down a moment when you saw our mission in action—when you personally witnessed how adaptive intelligence advanced human potential."

The sound of typing and scribbling filled the room. As people began to share, each story revealed a different facet of their mission.

James spoke about his brother with autism, how adaptive communication tools had opened new ways for him to express himself. "When I see 'advancing human potential,' I think of his first complete sentence using our interface."

Marcus described testing their neural interface with a paralyzed veteran. "She moved a robotic arm just by thinking. That's what 'adaptive intelligence' means to me: technology that adapts to human needs, not the other way around."

Stephanie shared how their collaboration tools had kept her connected to her team during chemotherapy. "I could contribute meaningfully even on my worst days. That's advancing human potential—making sure everyone can participate, regardless of circumstances."

In the corner of the room, the innovation principles visualization had evolved from a simple holographic display into something more tangible. Each principle now appeared on an interactive panel, lighting up when team members embodied it in their work.

Lee noticed a pattern forming. The principles weren't activating sequentially; they were lighting up in organic clusters, the various principles pulsing in harmony as teams moved naturally between them.

Each story added a layer of meaning to their mission, transforming abstract words into lived experiences. The mission hadn't changed, but their relationship to it had deepened.

When Missions Gain Traction

Later that afternoon, Lee found Ava in the Gardens. The rain had cleared, leaving the glass panels streaked with droplets that caught the emerging sunlight.

"I heard about your team meeting," she said, a knowing smile playing at the corners of her mouth. "Quite a different approach from your usual reorganization announcements."

Lee ran his hand through his hair, still processing the morning's events. "I took a risk. But something you said about making the mission personal... It got me thinking about why we really do this work."

"And how did the team respond?"

"Differently," Lee admitted. "After the meeting, James from Engineering pulled me aside. Turns out his brother uses assistive communication technology. He has three new ideas for features that could help users like him. James never mentioned this before."

"That's the power of personal mission," Ava said. "When people connect their personal why to the organization's purpose, innovation becomes natural. They're not just doing their jobs—they're pursuing their passion."

She pulled up the team's communication metrics again. The latest hour showed a 312 percent increase in collaborative discussions, with topics shifting from job listings to feature ideas and user impact stories.

"Remember," Ava added, "a mission statement that comes from above is just more corporate speak. But a mission that emerges from shared stories and personal meaning? That's a force for transformation."

Lee nodded, thinking about how different this felt from previous change initiatives. "We're not just reorganizing the company; we're reconnecting people with their purpose."

"Exactly. Because when mission becomes personal, change becomes purposeful." Ava smiled. "And that's how you break the chain of Apathy."

Principle 7: Make Your Mission Personal

When people connect their personal purpose to your
organizational mission, transformation becomes inevitable.

Key Takeaways & Considerations

Mission Versus Meaning: Corporate mission statements are just words until people find their personal connection to them. Transformation happens at the speed of meaning, not mandates.

From Prescription to Cocreation: Mission resonance comes from involvement, not announcement. Create space for individual interpretation and meaning making. Personal stakes in the mission drive innovation more than metrics.

Breaking the Chain of Apathy: Disconnection from purpose leads to change fatigue, but reconnecting with personal meaning reignites engagement.

The goal isn't to enforce a mission but to create conditions where personal connection to purpose can flourish. When people find their own meaning in the mission, transformation becomes not just possible but inevitable.

Put It into Practice: Rediscover Your Why

Ready to understand how and why you connected with your organization's mission? Tackle the **Mission Origin Story** exercise at changefluency.com/bookresources or scan the QR code. By exploring these questions, you'll uncover the authentic story that drives your commitment and gives meaning to your work. Take time to reflect deeply on each question, considering both emotional and practical aspects of your journey and connection to the mission.

Making Mission Personal

Organizations that successfully navigate transformation often share one key practice: They help employees discover their personal connections to the mission. Companies with strong purpose outperform the market by 5–7 percent per year. Here are three examples that illuminate different approaches:

Patagonia: Living the Mission

When Patagonia declares "We're in business to save our home planet," they don't just post it on walls—they create experiences that make it personal. Their Environmental Internships program allows every employee to take paid time working with environmental nonprofits, transforming abstract mission into lived experience.

Result: 89 percent of employees report feeling personally connected to the company's environmental mission, driving industry-leading retention and innovation.

Microsoft: Putting Mission into Personal Growth

Microsoft's mission, "to empower every person and every organization on the planet to achieve more," is a design brief for the employee experience. Every July, the company pauses normal work for OneWeek, a global festival anchored by the world's largest private hackathon. In 2019, more than 27,000 employees gathered across forty-five venues with thirty customer teams, "breaking something to make something." These customer-immersion days have become what engineers call their "impact days," giving each participant firsthand stories of how their code or prototype drives real-world achievement.

Result: Microsoft's latest internal "Good Deal" survey found that 65 percent of employees feel they get a fair exchange for their contribution—up three points in six months following recent culture-practice refreshes and OneWeek rollouts.

Cleveland Clinic: Creating Mission Through Moments

At Cleveland Clinic, every executive nursing meeting begins with a "Mission Moment"—a real patient story or thank-you letter shared by a nurse leader. As Cleveland Clinic's chief caregiver officer explained, pausing to hear these stories "serves as a reset for all of us... getting back to what it means to be a caregiver and why we are really here."

This kind of systematic meaning-making, which turns abstract values into tangible, personal examples, helps health care employees see the higher purpose in their day-to-day work.

Result: Such mission-driven engagement has measurable benefits. Research by Deloitte finds that "mission-driven" companies have 30 percent higher levels of innovation and 40 percent higher retention, and they tend to lead their industries (often ranking first or second in their market segment). In other words, organizations that consistently connect employees to a meaningful mission enjoy more loyal, motivated teams and stronger performance outcomes.

Key Patterns of Successful Organizations

Story Collection: Systematic gathering and sharing of mission impact stories.

Personal Experience: Creating opportunities for firsthand mission engagement.

Mission Metrics: Measuring both impact and personal connection to purpose.

These organizations succeed, not by changing their mission but by helping every employee discover their personal stake in it. They understand that mission statements become powerful when they become lived experiences, not just words.

13
Cultivate Contribution over Participation

We're Perfectly Participating

Lee's eyebrows furrowed as he studied Artemis' latest transformation metrics in his neural display.

The numbers painted a seemingly positive picture: 92 percent completion rate on AI training modules, 87 percent attendance at cross-functional meetings, 94 percent platform adoption across departments. Yet something felt fundamentally wrong. These metrics measured presence, not impact—like counting how many people showed up to a concert without asking if anyone enjoyed the music.

"Our metrics are all green," Lee said to Ava, gesturing at the holographic data floating between them. "So, why does it feel like we're losing ground?"

Ava studied the displays with focused intensity. "You're seeing our third chain of change in action: Competing Interests. When metrics drive behavior, people optimize for what's measured, not what matters."

She walked to the whiteboard, uncapping a marker with deliberate care. "Think about it. Engineering gets rewarded for feature releases, while Operations is measured on stability. Sales targets revenue growth, while Customer Success prioritizes satisfaction scores. Marketing chases brand metrics while Product focuses on user engagement. Everyone's doing their job, but are we moving forward together?"

The question hung in the air as Lee reflected on the morning's cross-functional meeting. The TechMinds team had attended—their participation rate was perfect—but they'd sat silently, clearly there only because it was required. Their bonuses were tied to integration milestones, not innovation outcomes.

"We've created perfect participation," Lee realized, "but killed genuine contribution."

Ava's eyes lit up with that familiar mix of challenge and possibility. "Ever heard of the starfish and the spider?"

"Is this one of your infamous nature metaphors I've been hearing about?" Lee rolled his eyes dramatically. "Next, you'll be telling me our organization should function like a colony of naked mole rats."

"Oh please." Ava smirked, crossing her arms. "Naked mole rats are for next quarter's transformation strategy. I'm pacing myself with the weird animal analogies."

Lee shook his head smiling, watching as she pulled up a new visualization in the air between them.

"In 2006, Ori Brafman and Rod Beckstrom wrote about two fundamentally different types of organizations," Ava explained. "Spider organizations and starfish organizations. If you cut off a spider's head, it dies. But if you cut off a starfish's arm, it doesn't just survive—it regenerates. The severed arm can even grow into a completely new starfish."

The Gardens' displays shifted to show these contrasting organizational structures. "Spider organizations are centralized, dependent on key leaders. When those leaders leave, the organization struggles. But starfish organizations?" She gestured, and the visualization showed a network of interconnected nodes. "They're built on contribution, not control. Every part can function independently while serving the whole."

Lee thought about Sarah's departure and its ripple effects. "We've been building a spider, haven't we? When Sarah left for Delta..."

"... the team struggled to maintain momentum," Ava finished. "Because we'd created a participation-focused structure where people were prompted to adopt and comply—instead of a contribution-focused network where anyone could step up and lead."

"But how do you actually build that kind of organization?" Lee asked, thinking of his sprawling team structures. "It's one thing to talk about decentralized networks, but—"

"Let me tell you about pizza," Ava interrupted, a smile playing at her lips. "Aria, show Amazon's two-pizza team documentation."

The display showed historical footage from Amazon's early days. "Jeff Bezos had a simple rule: No team should be larger than can be fed by two pizzas. The rule was about enabling genuine contribution. In small teams, everyone has to contribute. More importantly, everyone *can* contribute. There's no place to hide, no way to participate without creating value.

"But it's more than just team size," Ava continued. "Think about what happens in a two-pizza team. When there are only six to eight people in the room, the dynamic fundamentally changes. Communication becomes direct, ownership becomes clear, and most importantly—impact becomes visible."

The Gardens' displays shifted to show team interaction patterns. "In large groups, we see what psychologists call social loafing—people naturally contribute less when responsibility is diffused. But in small, empowered teams?" The visualization highlighted intense clusters of collaboration. "Every voice matters. Every contribution counts."

Lee studied the patterns, thinking about his own sprawling team meetings. "Is that why our standups feel so... performative lately?"

"Exactly." Ava nodded. "When you have thirty people in a standup, it becomes about reporting status—participation—rather than solving problems together—contribution. We've optimized for involvement at the expense of impact."

She turned to the whiteboard, writing:

Mindset shift from measuring attendance	→	**measuring impact**
Mindset shift from tracking completion	→	**tracking creation**
Mindset shift from rewarding presence	→	**rewarding purpose**

Innovation Principle 8: Cultivate Contribution over Participation

"You see," she continued, "the chain of Competing Interests isn't just about different departments having different goals. It's about the gap between what we measure and what matters. Between showing up and stepping up.

Between participating because we have to and contributing because we want to."

The Gardens' ambient displays shifted, showing new patterns of interaction: spontaneous collaborations between former rivals, innovative solutions emerging from unexpected corners, stories of impact shared across teams. These weren't the neat quantifiable metrics beloved by board members. They were messier, more organic indicators of real transformation.

"I've been thinking about what you said regarding the TechMinds integration," Lee said, watching the patterns evolve. "When we focused on participation metrics—getting them to attend our meetings, complete our onboarding, adopt our processes—we created resistance. But when we started recognizing their contributions, sharing their innovations, celebrating their unique perspectives..."

"...the walls between us and them started to dissolve," Ava finished. "Because contribution isn't about whose metrics win or whose processes dominate. It's about creating something meaningful together."

James materialized in their mixed reality space, his avatar carrying the same intensity he brought to in-person meetings. "The TechMinds team just shared something interesting," he began. "They've been tracking not just how many people use our new AI features but how they're enhancing them. Engineers are spontaneously contributing improvements; users are sharing unexpected applications. It's not just adoption; it's evolution."

Lee nodded, remembering how differently things had felt four months ago. Back then, they'd celebrated high participation numbers while missing the warning signs of disconnection that had led to Sarah's departure. Now, they were learning to spot the early signals of genuine transformation.

"Show me," Lee said.

James's neural interface expanded the visualization, revealing a web of contributions spreading across the organization. Like a starfish regenerating, each small team had begun creating and innovating independently while strengthening the whole. A customer service representative had discovered how to use their empathy algorithms to better support users in crisis. A junior developer had found a way to make their collaboration tools more accessible for neurodivergent team members. Each contribution had sparked others, creating chains of innovation that no training program could have prescribed.

"This is what we should be measuring," Lee realized. "Not just what people do because we ask them to, but what they create because they want to. Not how many people show up, but how they contribute when they do."

The shift was subtle but profound. Instead of tracking lagging indicators like platform usage statistics, survey response rates, and general participation numbers, Lee saw he should focus on leading indicators: the quality and frequency of voluntary contributions, the emergence of informal champions and advocates, instances of peer-to-peer knowledge sharing, spontaneous collaboration across silos, stories of impact being shared, questions and suggestions coming from unexpected voices.

Leading Versus Lagging Indicators

Common *lagging indicators* (measuring what has happened) might include number of people who completed training, survey response rates, platform usage statistics, customer satisfaction scores, revenue figures, employee turnover rates, meeting attendance numbers, and project completion rates.

Common *leading indicators* (predicting what might happen) might include quality and frequency of voluntary contributions, emergence of informal champions, instances of spontaneous cross-team collaboration, employee-initiated improvement suggestions, innovation submissions, stories of impact being shared unprompted, questions coming from unexpected voices, and examples of people living organizational values.

Lee considered Mark from Marketing, the Olympic gold medalist of fake participation. This guy showed up to every meeting with his laptop strategically angled—not for notes but to hide his record-breaking *Candy Crush* tournament. Mark's entire contribution vocabulary consisted of "great point," "let's circle back," and the occasional "I'm just thinking out loud here" when he unexpectedly got called on while reaching level 342. He'd perfected what his colleagues called the "thoughtful nod": a precise 72-degree head tilt that worked whether discussing quarterly results or the office microwave etiquette. Meanwhile, Stephanie might have missed a meeting or two but actually moved projects forward instead of just moving her avatar across a digital candy board.

The difference? Mark created the illusion of teamwork; Stephanie actually did the work.

Lee implemented a new recognition system. Each morning began with teams sharing not what they'd completed but what they'd contributed. The Gardens' ambient displays now highlighted innovation stories alongside metrics, giving equal weight to qualitative impact and quantitative results.

The effect was transformative. When people realized their contributions mattered—really mattered—they stopped simply participating and started actively creating. Cross-departmental collaboration flourished not because it was mandated but because it was meaningful.

A Milli Mentors

One morning, after they watched a particularly elegant solution emerge from collaboration between former competitors, Lee turned to Ava. "Thanks for mentoring me through all this," he said quietly.

Ava laughed, then replied with characteristic directness, "You don't need a mentor. What most of us need are a milli mentors—a thousand of 'em."

Lee mimicked the Lil Wayne song, "A milli a milli a milli."

"Haha, yes! We need an experienced sounding board for the particular situation that we're dealing with in that moment. For instance, remember when you were graduating from your master's program? At that time, you didn't need a mentor; you needed someone who could walk you through the experience of seeking employment after graduation. Three years into your role, you didn't need that person anymore, but you needed the perspective of someone who was in middle or upper management and had successfully navigated the political landscape of your organization to progress their career. I couldn't possibly be a mentor."

"Hmm, an experienced sounding board..." Lee considered that for a moment, seeing how it reflected the larger

Transformation spreads through champions, **not compliance.**

transformation they were creating—moving from hierarchical spider structures to networks of mutual contribution, akin to a starfish.

"Remember when I told you to measure what matters?" Ava asked, as they reviewed the contribution metrics.

"You mean yesterday?" Lee quipped.

"No, I mean three months ago, when we were focusing on breaking the Clutter and Chaos chain." She pulled up the historical visualization. "Look at how far we've come. First, we learned to see patterns in the noise. Then, we discovered how to harness wonder instead of certainty. We transformed our constraints into advantages. And now—"

"Now, we've made it personal so that our teams can contribute," Lee finished. "Each principle building on the last."

"It's not a checklist, Lee. It's a journey. And journeys change the traveler." She gestured toward the team collaboration spaces, where once-siloed groups now flowed between projects with natural fluency. "We didn't just implement principles; we became them."

The Gardens' systems registered a spike in collective energy as teams worldwide began their daily contribution sharing. Through the neural-link network, stories flowed in: A team in Singapore had adapted their empathy algorithms to better understand cultural nuances. Engineers in Seattle and former TechMinds developers in Bangalore had collaborated on a breakthrough in AI-human interaction. Each story built on the others, creating a tapestry of innovation far richer than any participation metric could capture.

Later, as the Gardens' systems recalibrated to normal operations, Lee studied the latest contribution patterns. Tomorrow would bring its own challenges: medical uncertainties, market pressures, the constant push of technological evolution. But today had shown him something crucial: Transformation spreads through champions, not compliance. And champions emerge when you recognize not just their participation but their contribution to something larger than themselves.

The Seattle skyline had darkened, but the Gardens still pulsed with activity. In the visualization, new patterns were already emerging, showing how tomorrow's innovations would grow from today's contributions. The living walls bloomed with fresh growth, responding to the energy of possibility.

Tomorrow would bring uncertainty. But today had shown that the strongest organizations, like the strongest people, don't just adapt to change—they contribute to it. They create it. They champion it. And in doing so, they transform not just metrics but meaning itself.

Principle 8:
Cultivate Contribution over Participation

Focus on what you collectively contribute.

Key Takeaways & Considerations

Focus On Leading Indicators Instead of Lagging Indicators: Move beyond participation metrics; traditional metrics like attendance rates, platform usage, and survey completions only measure presence, not impact. True transformation requires measuring meaningful contribution. *Lagging indicators* (participation numbers, usage statistics) tell you what happened. *Leading indicators* (voluntary contributions, peer-to-peer sharing, innovation stories) predict what's possible.

Recognition Drives Replication: When you celebrate meaningful contributions, you create a culture where people strive to contribute rather than merely comply.

Focus On Contribution, Not Participation: Contribution-focused environments naturally break down silos, as people connect through shared purpose rather than mandatory participation. By focusing on contribution over compliance, you create space for natural leaders and innovators to emerge organically.

Put It into Practice: Measure Your Impact

The **Impact Measurement Framework** helps organizations shift their focus from tracking activities to measuring outcomes that actually matter. Many organizations struggle with transformation because they're looking at the wrong metrics. This framework helps you identify, measure, and amplify the indicators that truly drive transformation.

Get the framework at changefluency.com/bookresources or scan the QR code.

Top Ten Ways to Know Your Company Needs Transformation

1 Your team's innovation pipeline looks more constipated than creative.

2 Meetings are where ideas go to die a death by a thousand PowerPoint slides.

3 Your company's mission statement requires a PhD to understand.

4 Your competitors are using AI, and your team is still trying to figure out how to unmute themselves on Zoom.

5 The company values poster in the breakroom is just a list of words that no one remembers... except the intern who was forced to memorize them for onboarding.

6 Every new initiative is met with a collective sigh so deep it alters local weather patterns.

7 The office coffee is stronger than your leadership's commitment to change.

8 Your IT department still insists that Internet Explorer is a "perfectly fine" browser.

9 The most consistent company-wide decision is where to order lunch from.

10 You have a change management team, but their most-used phrase is "That's just how we've always done it."

14
Create
with Care

Unexpected Gestures

Lee glared at the Gardens' BaristaBot, which had somehow managed to interpret his request for "a little extra caffeine" as "replace coffee with motor oil."

"No, I don't want to rate my experience on a scale of one to five," he snapped at the cheerful metallic face. "I want coffee that doesn't qualify as hazardous waste."

BaristaBot pepped back, "Your feedback makes us better!" which only deepened Lee's longing for the human baristas who once occupied this space. At least they knew when a rough morning warranted an extra shot without asking.

Lee's neural display flickered with the latest metrics: Delta's quantum processing capabilities now exceeded theirs by 500 percent, yet somehow Artemis' user retention had started trending upward. Something fundamental had shifted but not what he'd expected.

"You look deep in thought this morning. Worried about something?" Ava observed, settling beside him.

Lee touched the small scar near his temple, a habit he'd developed since the surgery. "Reflecting actually. I was thinking about how different this journey has been from my first battle with cancer."

Ava's eyebrows lifted, her attention sharpening. "Your first battle?"

"I never told you about that, did I?" Lee's gaze drifted to the Seattle skyline. "I was twelve. We'd just moved here from Singapore. Everything was new: the city, the school, the language. Then came the diagnosis." He paused, remembering. "Outside of my family and my care team, I went through it mostly alone. Back then, that seemed like strength—keeping it all inside, not burdening others."

The Gardens' living walls pulsed gently to reflect the emotional weight of the memory.

"But this time, with the pituitary tumor…" Lee shook his head. "I decided to do something different. Started telling people, one by one. Family first, then close friends. Each conversation was hard in its own way. Everyone had their practiced responses: 'Oh, I'm so sorry' or 'You'll beat this' or 'Let me know if you need anything.'"

"But one of my friends showed up differently. His name is Jeff. There we were at Lola's for brunch, and I started with my usual spiel. 'Jeff, I don't know how else to tell you this, but I have a tumor in my head.'"

Lee's voice softened. "He didn't say anything. Time froze and stood still as he took the information in. Didn't offer advice or platitudes. He just sat with it for a moment, really sat with it. Then, he reached across the table and held my hand.

"And we have never held hands before." Lee laughed.

"In that moment, the millimeter tumor felt like a million-pound mountain that I had been trying to hold up. My mind flashed forward into the future, picturing everything I so desperately wanted to witness: Grace walking across the stage at her high school graduation, our eyes meeting as she turns to give me that cheeky 'I did it!' look; catching Chloe blazing around a parking lot as she gets her license at sixteen; everything from walking them down the aisle to the moment Teresa and I find out that we're grandparents." Lee's eyes filled with tears as he choked back his words.

"Jeff squeezed my hand. And with that small, but unexpected gesture, he *created a moment with care.*"

Lee wrinkled his nose and sniffed, pausing to recollect himself as he wiped his eyes gently.

"We get to work on the most transformative technology in our world today. Yet the most transformative moments for me over the past two years have not been with *technology* but with *people.*"

He gestured to his neural display, where Delta's latest quantum processing benchmarks still flickered. "After all our work on emotional intelligence algorithms and neural interfaces, Jeff's simple act of human connection reinforces for me what we're really building here at Artemis."

Ava leaned back, raising an eyebrow. "So, what you're saying is . . . our multibillion-dollar AI platform got outperformed by a guy named Jeff at brunch?"

"Technically, Jeff doesn't even have a neural interface," Lee shot back with a grin. "Imagine what he could do with our budget."

"Jeff just out-innovated our entire R & D department with one hand squeeze," Ava quipped, her eyes sparkling with mischief.

The Gardens' displays showed their latest user engagement patterns, but Lee saw them differently now. "You know what's ironic? In trying to compete with Delta's quantum processing power, we'd almost missed the most powerful innovation of all: the courage to create with care.

"That single moment of care sparked a deeper bond. It taught me something crucial about differentiation in our increasingly automated world: When everything else can be replicated, *care becomes the ultimate differentiator.*"

The Power of Care in a High-Tech World

Ava tossed a stress ball up in the air.

"You know what's interesting about the race to catch up to Delta's success?" she asked, tracking the ball as she continued. "Everyone's focusing on their technology, their rapid user growth, their market dominance. But they're asking the wrong question."

She paused, as the morning light caught the steam rising from her coffee. "The real question isn't 'How do we match their features?' It's 'How do we create something people will care about as deeply as we do?'"

Ava waved away their latest user engagement metrics from the display. "Let me tell you about another company that discovered the power of care in transformation. When Calvin McDonald took over lululemon in 2018, everyone expected him to focus on rapid expansion and efficiency. Instead, he asked a different question: 'How do we scale care without diluting it?'"

Lee leaned forward, seeing parallels to their own challenge with Delta. "What did they discover?"

"Three things," Ava replied, sipping her coffee. "First, care can be systematic without being automated. They developed rigorous processes for product development but maintained their obsessive attention to human experience.

Designers didn't just test fabrics in labs; they sat through entire yoga classes, observing how people actually moved and felt.

"Second," she continued, "care should enhance technology, not be replaced by it. When COVID-19 hit and retailers rushed to automate everything, lululemon took a different approach. They used digital tools to strengthen human connections, not eliminate them. Their mobile app didn't just process transactions; it connected customers with local instructors and communities."

"And third?" Lee asked, thinking about their own technology choices.

"Care becomes contagious when it's authentic. Instead of just translating their marketing for international expansion, they spent a year understanding how movement and wellness were viewed differently in each culture. In China, they discovered yoga wasn't about exercise—it was about finding peace in chaotic urban life. So, they adapted, creating early morning meditation sessions in teahouses instead of just replicating their Western model."

The Gardens' ambient displays showed lululemon's growth: from $3.3 billion in 2018 to over $8 billion in 2023. But more striking were the stories of impact: communities formed, lives transformed, connections strengthened.

"But here's what matters most," Ava said, her voice softening. "In a world where any company can access powerful technology, you're right: Care becomes the ultimate differentiator. When Jeff held your hand at Lola's, he didn't follow a script or best practice. He simply cared enough to be present, to create a moment of genuine connection. That's what we need to do at scale."

Lee stood, holding out his hand to grab a marker for the whiteboard. "So, if that's what we need to do—build care

In an AI-powered world of increasing automation, **care becomes the key differentiator.**

into our systems without losing its soul—I think I know our final Innovation Principle."

Ava smiled, handing Lee the blue marker:

Mindset shift from optimizing for efficiency → **optimizing for impact**

Innovation Principle 9: Create with Care

He paused, marker hovering over the board. "You know what I've realized? Creating with care isn't just about being nice—it's about being intentional. Every decision we make either strengthens or weakens human connection."

"Exactly." Ava nodded. "Any idea on the three essential questions that would help guide us in living out this innovation principle?"

Lee pondered, then began whiteboarding:

Does this enhance or diminish human connection?

"Think about Delta's quantum processing," Lee reflected. "Yes, it's faster. Yes, it's more powerful. But what we're seeing in our user data is fascinating—people aren't just looking for speed. They're looking for understanding."

The Gardens' displays shifted to show recent user feedback: teams reporting deeper collaboration, better communication, stronger relationships through their platform. "Our slower processing actually creates space for more meaningful interaction," Lee noted. "Every feature we build either brings people closer together or pushes them further apart." Next, he wrote the second question:

Are we remaining authentic to what we believe in (our values)?

"This one hits home," Lee said, thinking about their journey. "When we were chasing Delta's capabilities, we weren't just compromising our technology—we were compromising our values. We believe AI should enhance human potential, not replace it."

Ava gestured to their product road map floating in the ambient display. "Values aren't just platitudes; they're decision-making tools. When TechMinds integrated their emotional AI with our collaboration platform, it wasn't just a technical achievement. It was an expression of our shared belief that technology should serve humanity, not the other way around."

Lee jotted down the third question:

> How well does the voice of our customer match our product strategy?

The Gardens' smart glass filled with user stories— not metrics or feature requests but real experiences of how Artemis' platform had impacted lives. A teacher using their emotional AI to better understand struggling students. A global team bridging cultural differences through their live translation tool. A health care provider maintaining human connection in virtual consultations by identifying patient emotions for the doctor to empathize with.

"This is where most companies get it wrong," Ava observed. "They listen to customer feedback, but they filter it through their existing strategy. Real care means letting customer voices reshape your strategy entirely."

Lee nodded, thinking of Jeff again. "It's like that moment at Lola's. Jeff didn't just hear my words about the tumor; he felt the weight behind them. He let my experience reshape his response."

"And that's the key to scaling care," Ava added. "It's not about creating processes that simulate care. It's about creating environments where authentic care can flourish."

The Gardens' living walls pulsed with new patterns as Lee began mapping out how these questions would transform their approach, seeing how each encapsulated the previous innovation principles:

- **Product Development:** Every feature evaluated not just for technical performance but for its impact on human connection.

- **Team Structures:** Small, autonomous groups that could form deeper bonds and respond more authentically to user needs.

- **Success Metrics:** New measurements focused on depth of engagement rather than just breadth of adoption.

- **Decision-Making:** Values-based frameworks that prioritized human impact over pure efficiency.

Care as a Competitive Advantage

"You know what's remarkable?" Lee said, stepping back from the whiteboard. "These aren't just nice-to-have questions. In a world where AI can replicate almost anything, authentic care becomes our most sustainable competitive advantage."

"It allows us to develop fluency in recognizing and creating new market spaces," Ava added, bringing up a visual comparison between Delta's and Artemis' approaches. "Just as language fluency allows you to express complex thoughts without conscious translation, market fluency enables you to see opportunities others miss.

"While most companies develop rigid proficiency in competing within established markets, those with true fluency can seamlessly shift between different market contexts, creating innovations that both stick with users and stand out from competitors.

"Delta's stuck trying to perfect their grammar in a language everyone already speaks. We're becoming fluent in a dialect that resonates more deeply with how people actually want to connect."

Ava smiled, watching as the teams worldwide began joining their morning session through the neural-link network. "Care at scale isn't an oxymoron. It's an imperative. But it only works when it's genuine, grounded in values, and deeply connected to the people we serve."

Through the Gardens' smart glass, Seattle's tech corridor was coming alive with morning activity. Somewhere out there, Delta's quantum processors were setting new speed records. But as Lee prepared to share these insights with his global team, he felt something he hadn't experienced since the crisis began: certainty. Not about their technology or their market position but about their purpose. In a world racing to be faster, they would be the ones who cared enough to go deeper.

"Ready to share this with the team?" Ava asked.

"Actually," Lee replied, "I think I'll start by asking them a question: 'When was the last time someone's care made a difference in your life?' Because before we can create with care, we need to understand what care really means to each of us."

The Gardens' ambient systems registered a surge of energy as team members began joining from around the world, each bringing their own understanding of care, ready to help build something that mattered not just because it *worked* well but because it *cared* well.

The Path Forward

"The irony," Ava concluded, setting down her now-empty coffee cup, "is that in our rush to keep up with Delta, we risk losing the very thing that could set us apart: our capacity to care deeply about the experiences we create."

Lee was beginning to see how this applied to Artemis' challenge. It wasn't about matching Delta's technology or speed to market. It was about creating something people would care about as deeply as they did.

In a world of increasing automation and artificial intelligence, the companies that thrive won't be those that create the most efficient solutions—they'll be those that create the most thoughtful ones. Because while technology can help us move faster, only care can help us move people.

Principle 9: Create with Care

In a world where technology can replicate
almost anything, authentic human care becomes
your greatest competitive advantage.

Key Takeaways & Considerations

In an AI-powered world of increasing automation, care becomes the key differentiator. The gap between good and great lies in how deeply you care about the human experience. Care cannot be mandated, but it can be cultivated. Cultivate care through the three care questions framework:

1 Does this *enhance* or *diminish* human connection?

2 Are we remaining *authentic* to what we believe in?

3 How well does the *voice of our customer* match our product strategy?

Creating with care isn't about moving slowly. It's about moving thoughtfully.

Put It into Practice: Care Audit

One of the hardest things to do is to systematically evaluate and enhance how care manifests in your organization's practices, products, and interactions. Rather than trying to institutionalize care through rigid processes, the **Care Audit** helps you identify opportunities to create conditions where authentic care can flourish at scale.

Take action at changefluency.com/ bookresourcesor scan the QR code.

When Service Transcends Strategy

Creating Care at Scale: The challenge for modern organizations isn't only creating with care, it's doing so at scale. This requires a fundamental shift in how we think about innovation.

From Features to Feelings: Instead of asking "What features can we add?" successful organizations ask, "How do we want people to feel?" When Apple designed AirPods, they didn't just create wireless earbuds; they obsessed over the design of the case, too, such as the color, form, noise of a click, and magnetic force of the case—all of the little details that elicit a sense of joy when using it.

From Efficiency to Experience: Rather than optimizing solely for speed, optimize for memorability. Trader Joe's, for instance, deliberately maintains smaller stores with fewer products than conventional supermarkets. This creates an experience that feels more like discovery in a boutique than regular grocery shopping.

From Copying to Creating: Instead of following best practices, establish next practices. When everyone else was creating automated customer service systems, Zappos chose to remove time limits from customer calls. Their longest customer service call lasted ten hours and forty-three minutes—and they celebrated it!

Epilogue

AN HOUR NORTH OF SEATTLE, as the afternoon sun danced across the waters of Semiahmoo, the inlet bordering the US-Canada border, Lee watched his daughter Grace guide her drone in graceful arcs above the shoreline. Her face displayed the focused determination he recognized in himself when he looked in the mirror each morning.

"It's getting much better, Dad!" Grace called out, her eyes never leaving the drone's flight path. "Seventy-five percent accuracy now! Ms. Rodriguez says they might use it in other classrooms, too, not just for the neurodivergent kids."

Teresa settled beside him on the weathered driftwood log, handing him a thermos of coffee. Audrey was nearby, building intricate sandcastle structures.

"Penny for your thoughts?" Teresa asked, bumping his shoulder gently with hers.

"Just thinking about everything that's changed this year."

"The tumor?"

Lee ran his hand up the back of his head slowly. The tumor that once felt like a million-pound mountain had become, surprisingly, his greatest teacher. Through it, he learned their nine principles of innovation weren't just organizational strategies; they were universal truths about human growth.

"That. Artemis. Me." He took a slow sip of coffee. "When I first got the diagnosis, all I could think about was what I might lose. Every scenario I ran was about loss. Every metric I tracked was about survival."

A discreet vibration against his wrist signaled an incoming video message, the neural interface he'd forgotten to silence. With a quick gesture, he opened it—Elena.

Unlike the panic-stricken video call that had started this journey, her tone now carried something close to admiration. "The board is impressed. So is our lead investor. Your approach to human-centered AI has differentiated us in unexpected ways. Well done."

Lee smiled faintly, dismissing the message without responding. There was a time when Elena's approval would have been the highlight of his week. Now, it felt like one data point among many: important, but not defining.

"Good news?" Teresa asked.

"Board approval," he said. "Apparently our human-centered approach is working."

They watched as Grace's drone wobbled, then stabilized, capturing images of the waves gently crashing against the shore.

"It's funny," Lee continued. "I approached both problems the same way at first—Delta's disruption and the tumor. I wanted certainty. Control. To eliminate the chaos." He gestured toward Grace. "But look at her. Her neural network fails 25 percent of the time, and she's not worried about optimization or benchmarks. She's excited about what it *does* create."

Teresa nodded. "She told me it's helping kids who have trouble reading emotions."

"That's what I missed before," Lee said. "At Artemis, we were so focused on what we might lose to Delta that we couldn't see what we might create instead. We measured success by how much market share we could defend rather than how much human potential we could unlock."

Audrey ran up, sand covering her knees, holding out a small structure she'd made. "Look, Dad! It's our house, but with a garden on the roof like at your work!"

Lee examined it carefully. "That's incredible, sweetheart. I love how you've reimagined it."

As Audrey ran back to her construction site, another notification appeared: Maya was sending him the latest metrics. Unlike the crisis-tracking displays that once dominated their meetings, these dashboards told a different story: user retention up 42 percent, team innovation submissions at record highs, and most telling—stories of impact flowing through their neural-link network daily.

"Our principles are working," Maya's message noted. "Who would've thought that operations would be celebrating slower processing speeds? But the data's clear. Our human-centered approach is creating deeper engagement than Delta's quantum processing could ever achieve."

Lee smiled, remembering Maya's initial skepticism. The woman who once measured success in milliseconds had gone from their biggest operational critic to their most powerful advocate, transforming constraints into competitive advantages across their infrastructure.

Just as he closed Maya's message, Ava was requesting a video call.

Lee glanced apologetically at his wife.

"Go ahead," Teresa urged. "I know you've been waiting to hear from her."

With a gesture, Lee accepted the call. Ava's face materialized in his field of vision, SEATAC's departure gates visible behind her. She was starting her sabbatical with a trip to Argentina.

"Ready for Grace's science fair next week?" Ava asked, as she shifted her midnight-blue carry-on suitcase to the side and slipped her backpack through the handle to sit on top.

Lee smiled, glancing at Grace as she showed a younger child how to interact with the drone. "She's already dreaming up what she might create next."

"The same wisdom we discovered through crisis," Ava observed. "That innovation isn't about processing power but processing purpose."

"How's everything at the Gardens?" Lee asked.

Ava smiled. "You should see it. The living walls have never looked more vibrant. It's like they're responding to the energy shift. Teams are wondering together, not just working together."

Lee thought about how the Gardens transformed from a space for crisis management to a living laboratory for human-centered innovation.

"You know what I've realized?" Lee said, watching the teams share their personal connections to Artemis' mission. "When we started this journey, you told me that our relationship with disruption determines our capacity for transformation."

"I remember." Ava nodded.

"I now understand what that means. It's not about processing disruption faster or more efficiently. It's about processing it more deeply—with more care, more wonder, more humanity."

Ava smiled. "And that's the final transformation: from seeing disruption as something to manage to seeing it as something to embrace. When we create with care, disruption becomes opportunity."

A voice sounded in the departures terminal: "United Flight 306 is now boarding for Buenos Aires. Please head to gate C34."

Our relationship with disruption determines our **capacity for transformation.**

"Sounds like you're up, Ava." Lee smiled appreciatively at her. "I'll try not to burn the place down while you're gone."

Ava lifted her hand to her temple in a playful salute. "Que será, será."

With a quick wave, Ava was gone.

Teresa pulled Lee to a stand. They began to head to the shoreline where their daughters were playing, Lee deep in thought.

Artemis now had all nine principles in action. They'd learned to zoom out to see patterns others missed, to evolve their vision through cocreation, to work in wonder rather than demand certainty. They'd made strategic sacrifices, leveraged their limits, painted a bigger canvas. They'd made their mission personal, cultivated contribution over participation, and most importantly—they were now creating with care.

As Lee glanced up, he saw Jeff's car round the bend leading up to the inlet. His friend's simple act of holding his hand after his diagnosis had become more than a moment of care—it had become Artemis' template for innovation. In an age of artificial intelligence, they had discovered that authentic human connection is the ultimate differentiator.

As Grace's drone captured the family moment from above, Lee realized something fundamental: Sometimes, the greatest innovation isn't in what we create but in how we help each other become more fully human.

Back in Seattle, the Gardens' living walls bloomed with new growth, their patterns a reminder that in this age of intelligence, our most profound innovation lies not in our technology but in our humanity.

And that's a disruption worth decoding.

Acknowledgments

TO MY WIFE, TERESA, who made this possible by rooting for me every step of the way. I'll never forget the moment at 1 a.m., wiped from a long day of work, parenting, and writing when I stumbled upon the "Bestselling Author in 2025" Post-it you left for me. Your belief in me has always been so resolute, so surefooted, so unwavering, which has meant the world to me on days where I have been anything but.

To my daughters, Madison and Chloe, you have been and continue to be the best role models for me to work in wonder. Through you, I've developed the deep belief that the ability to imagine possibility is what reshapes the world.

To Jeff, the audiences I speak to around the world have been moved by you—thank you for bringing the human connection to our friendship.

To my mom, thanks for showing me what agape parenthood looks like; you've been the best parent one could ask for. #AG2G

To Mandy Gill, your advice about plowing through the first draft to get to the substantive edit was exactly what I needed to gain traction—allowing me to spend more time unpacking the metaphors, humor, and stories that would capture my point of view. Thank you for being such a huge cheerleader throughout this whole process.

To Karen Ball, when I was just trying to figure out whether I should make the leap into writing my first book, you handed me a journal that kept me accountable. You didn't have to do that, but you ignited the confidence to move forward. Thank you.

To Eric Termuende, I say this to you every time we hang out, but you continue to be the single person that has changed the trajectory of my speaking career the most. Your generosity in giving and heart for seeing others succeed is a true testament to your character. Thanks for changing my life—you unlocked the path that allows me to live and evolve my dream daily.

To the Speakers Spotlight team, thanks for taking a bet on me. You've changed my life in ways that I could never have imagined. Marnie, your ability to see the potential in others is a true gift. Can't wait to see where we build to next.

To Scott, Jesse, and the rest of the Page Two publishing team, sorry for backtracking on not writing a parable. It was the baby bursting at the seams that just had to come into the world. The trust you placed in me was exactly what I needed to take the creative reins and run with it.

Appendix

Get your downloadable PDF of the Appendix and Glossary at changefluency.com/bookresources.

Innovation Principles at a Glance

Principle	Mindset Shift	Key Application
1. Zoom Out to Zoom In	From clutter and chaos → clarity	Analyze patterns in the noise before focusing on solutions
2. Evolve Your Vision	From comfort with status quo → desire to grow	Cocreate vision through diverse perspectives
3. Work in Wonder	From seeking certainty → embracing curiosity	Use the Cone of Possibilities to explore multiple futures
4. Strategy Is Sacrifice	From adding more → deleting for differentiation	Make deliberate choices about what to eliminate

Innovation Principles at a Glance

Principle	Mindset Shift	Key Application
5. Leverage Your Limits	From limits as obstacles → limits as catalysts	Transform constraints into competitive advantages
6. Paint a Bigger Canvas	From competing in markets → creating new markets	Expand your TAM instead of fighting for market share
7. Make Your Mission Personal	From mission as statement → mission as story	Connect organizational purpose to individual meaning
8. Cultivate Contribution over Participation	From measuring attendance → measuring impact	Focus on meaningful contributions rather than mere presence
9. Create with Care	From optimizing for efficiency → optimizing for impact	Make authentic human connection your differentiator

The Five Chains of Change at a Glance

Chain	Level	Description	Key Indicators
Clutter and Chaos	Organizational	Multiple competing priorities and constantly changing directions	Teams suffering from tyranny of the urgent; inability to prioritize; reactive rather than proactive decision-making
Comfort with Status Quo	Individual	Personal attachment to current systems and processes	Resistance phrases like "That's not how we do things around here"; preference for incremental improvements over bold changes
Competing Interests	Organizational and Team	Different departments having conflicting goals and metrics	Siloed thinking; competition for resources; misaligned incentives; teams optimizing for their metrics at expense of others

The Five Chains of Change at a Glance

Chain	Level	Description	Key Indicators
Constraints	Organizational	Limited resources (financial, time, talent, competency)	Resource scarcity; capability gaps; technology limitations; bandwidth restrictions
Apathy	Individual	Disengagement due to change fatigue, burnout, or frustration	Declining innovation submissions; perfunctory participation; cynicism in meetings

Notes

3. Dancing with Disruption

41   *"Seventy percent of those transformations"*: Jon Garcia, "Common Pitfalls in Transformations: A Conversation with Jon Garcia," McKinsey & Company, March 29, 2022, https://www.mckinsey.com/capabilities/transformation/our-insights/common-pitfalls-in-transformations-a-conversation-with-jon-garcia.

46   *The average organization undergoes three major transformations*: Michael Mankins and Patrick Litre, "Transformations That Work," *Harvard Business Review*, May–June 2024, https://hbr.org/2024/05/transformations-that-work.

4. Customer Exodus

63   *about 77 percent of employees*: State of the Global Workplace 2023 Report (Gallup, 2023).

63   *an estimated $7.8 trillion annually*: State of the Global Workplace 2022 Report (Gallup, 2022).

5. Zoom Out to Zoom In

73   *Revenue had plunged from $3.2 billion*: Wikipedia, "Video Game Crash of 1983," last edited July 6, 2025, 01:49 (UTC), https://en.wikipedia.org/wiki/Video_game_crash_of_1983.

75   *An astounding 118.69 million units*: Nintendo, "Dedicated Video Game Sales Units," last updated March 31, 2025, https://www.nintendo.co.jp/ir/en/finance/hard_soft/index.html.

76   *They identified usability challenges*: Wikipedia, "Extreme Users," last edited June 13, 2025, 03:14 (UTC), https://en.wikipedia.org/wiki/Extreme_users; Chris Kohler, "Iwata: 'Society

Will Be More Accommodating' to Games Post-Wii," *Wired*, October 16, 2006, https://www.wired.com/2006/10/iwata-society-w/.

77   *over 152 million units sold globally*: Nintendo, "Dedicated Video Game Sales Units."

6. Evolve Your Vision

91   *Brian Chesky, Airbnb's CEO*: Stanford Graduate School of Business, "Brian Chesky, Co-Founder and CEO of Airbnb: Designing a 10-Star Experience," YouTube video, February 27, 2023, https://www.youtube.com/watch?v=V6h_EDcj12k.

98   *"healthy dissatisfaction with the status quo"*: Dan Schwabel, "Mars CEO Grant Reid: Maintaining a Corporate Culture over 100 Years," *Forbes*, November 10, 2017, https://www.forbes.com/sites/danschawbel/2017/11/10/mars-ceo-grant-reid-maintaining-a-corporate-culture-over-100-years; Andrew Edgecliffe-Johnson, "Mars' Outgoing CEO on Succession, Family Businesses and Eating His Own Dog Food," *Financial Times*, September 29, 2022, https://www.ft.com/content/1bca0b45-4c86-4be2-b61a-b506a33a0e58.

100   *"[Our five] principles are the glue that holds us together"*: "Nichol MacManus, "110 Years of Family Business Ownership: A Conversation with Victoria Mars, Former Chairman and First Corporate Ombudsman of Mars," Insights, Brown Brothers Harriman, June 2, 2021, https://www.bbh.com/us/en/insights/capital-partners-insights/110-years-of-family-business-ownership-a-conversation-with-victoria-mars.html.

7. Work in Wonder

106   *they were losing $1 million a day*: Colin Baker, "How LEGO Rebuilt Its Empire Brick by Brick," *Leaders*, May 17, 2023, https://leaders.com/articles/business/lego/; "Innovation Almost Bankrupted LEGO—Until It Rebuilt with a Better Blueprint," Knowledge at Wharton, July 18, 2012, https://knowledge.wharton.upenn.edu/article/innovation-almost-bankrupted-lego-until-it-rebuilt-with-a-better-blueprint/; "LEGO Success Story: How the Toy Giant Stacked Its Way Back from $800 Million Debt to a Billion-Dollar Empire," *The Economic Times*, April 3, 2025, https://economictimes.indiatimes.com/news/new-updates/lego-success-story-how-the-toy-giant-stacked-its-way-back-from-800-million-debt-to

-a-billion-dollar-empire-just-1-question-changed-everything/
articleshow/119942943.cms.

108 *"Studies show that successful language learners have high 'ambiguity tolerance'"*: Miao Yu, Hongliang Wang, and Guoping Xia, "The Review on the Role of Ambiguity of Tolerance and Resilience on Students' Engagement," *Frontiers in Psychology* 12 (2022): 828894, https://doi.org/10.3389/fpsyg.2021.828894.

113 *First came Mindstorms in 1998*: Margaret K. Evans, "Member Collaboration: LEGO Mindstorms," MIT Media Lab, December 12, 2016, https://www.media.mit.edu/posts/member-collaboration-lego-s-mindstorms.

121 *nearly 1,500 artists generated over $1 million*: "Loud & Clear: Our Annual Music Economics Report," Spotify, March 2025, https://loudandclear.byspotify.com/.

8. Emergency

133 *"Don't wait for certainty"*: Chris Barton, interview with the author.

9. Strategy Is Sacrifice

139 *Toyota's 2024 strategic decisions*: Dominic Magee, *The Toyota Way: 14 Management Principles from the World's Greatest Manufacturer* (McGraw Hill, 2004).

139 *infrastructure and technology weren't ready for mass EV adoption*: Neal E. Boudette, "Toyota's Hybrid-First Strategy Is Delivering Big Profits," *The New York Times*, March 9, 2024, https://www.nytimes.com/2024/03/09/business/toyotas-hybrid-electic-vehicles.html.

139 *In 2025, Toyota announced a partnership with NVIDIA*: Rebecca Bellan, "Toyota's Next-Generation Cars Will Be Built with NVIDIA Supercomputers and Operating System," *TechCrunch*, January 6, 2025, https://techcrunch.com/2025/01/06/toyotas-next-generation-cars-will-be-built-with-nvidia-supercomputers-and-operating-system/; NVIDIA, "Toyota, Aurora and Continental Join Growing List of NVIDIA Partners Rolling Out Next-Generation Highly Automated and Autonomous Vehicle Fleets," press release, January 6, 2025, https://nvidianews.nvidia.com/news/toyota-aurora-continental-nvidia-drive.

141   *Toyota picked a core offering*: Market projections for 2035 are completely speculative and based on historical trends up to 2025.

143   *one-way and two-way doors*: Startup Archive, "Jeff Bezos Explains One-Way Door Decisions and Two-Way Door Decisions," YouTube, January 14, 2024, https://youtu.be/rxsd0Qa_QkM.

143   *We often treat reversible decisions as irreversible ones*: Startup Archive, "Jeff Bezos Explains One-Way Door Decisions and Two-Way Door Decisions."

10. Leverage Your Limits

154   *Costco's Kirkland Signature*: Costco brought in $52B in revenue in 2023, just ahead of Nike by $1B. Phil Wahba, "How Costco Built Its $56 Billion Kirkland Store Brand That's Bigger Than Nike and Coca-Cola," *Fortune*, June 4, 2024, https://fortune.com/2024/06/04/costco-kirkland-store-brand-nike-coca-cola.

155   *FEDCO's business model*: Karen Newell Young, "Discount Stores in County Proliferate: A Profile of Fedco," *Los Angeles Times*, February 19, 1988, https://www.latimes.com/archives/la-xpm-1988-02-19-li-29759-story.html; Jesús Sanchez and Abigail Goldman, "Fedco to Seek Chapter 11 Protection, Close Doors," *Los Angeles Times*, July 10, 1999, https://www.latimes.com/archives/la-xpm-1999-jul-10-fi-54607-story.html.

12. Make Your Mission Personal

187   *"Did you know that 92 percent of Gen Z employees"*: "2025 Gen Z and Millennial Survey: Growth and the Pursuit of Money, Meaning, and Well-Being," Deloitte Touche Tohmatsu Limited, 2025, 4, https://www.deloitte.com/content/dam/assets-shared/docs/campaigns/2025/2025-genz-millennial-survey.pdf.

187   *Deloitte's 2024 Gen Z and Millennial Survey*: "2024 Gen Z and Millennial Survey: Living and Working with Purpose in a Transforming World," Deloitte Global, https://www.deloitte.com/content/dam/assets-shared/docs/campaigns/2024/deloitte-2024-genz-millennial-survey.pdf.

198   *Companies with strong purpose outperform the market*: Arne Gast, Pablo Illanes, Nina Probst, Bill Schaninger, and Bruce Simpson, "Purpose: Shifting from Why to How," McKinsey & Company, 2022, https://www.mckinsy.com/capabilities/

people-and-organizational-performance/our-insights/
purpose-shifting-from-why-to-how.

198   *89 percent of employees report feeling personally connected*:
"Fortune 100 Best Companies to Work for 2023,"
Great Place to Work, https://www.greatplacetowork.com/
best-workplaces/100-best/2023.

198   *Microsoft's mission*: "About," Microsoft, https://www.microsoft
.com/en-us/about.

198   *In 2019, more than 27,000 employees*: Larry Carroll, "At the
Microsoft Global Hackathon, Customers Break Something
to Make Something," Microsoft, July 25, 2019, https://news
.microsoft.com/source/features/digital-transformation/
at-the-microsoft-global-hackathon-customers-break
-something-to-make-something/.

199   *Microsoft's latest internal "Good Deal" survey*: Ashley Stewart,
"Internal Microsoft Survey Shows Employees Are Slightly Less
Grumpy About Pay," *Business Insider*, March 11, 2025, https://
www.businessinsider.com/microsoft-worker-poll-65-say
-working-there-is-good-deal-2025-3.

199   *every executive nursing meeting*: "Remembering What's
Most Important: Nurse Leaders Start Meetings with
'Mission Moments,'" Cleveland Clinic, September 23, 2020,
https://consultqd.clevelandclinic.org/remembering-whats
-most-important-nurse-leaders-start-meetings-with-mission
-moments.

199   *Research by Deloitte finds that "mission-driven" companies*:
"Becoming Irresistible: A New Model for Employee
Engagement," *Deloitte Review* 16, January 27, 2015, https://
www.deloitte.com/us/en/insights/topics/talent/employee
-engagement-strategies.html.

13. Cultivate Contribution over Participation

202   *"In 2006, Ori Brafman and Rod Beckstrom"*: Ori Brafman
and Rod A. Beckstrom, *The Starfish and The Spider: The
Unstoppable Power of Leaderless Organizations* (Portfolio, 2006).

203   *"Jeff Bezos had a simple rule"*: Brad Stone, *The Everything Store:
Jeff Bezos and the Age of Amazon* (Little, Brown and Company,
2013), 129.

204 *"what psychologists call social loafing"*: Williams Latané, Kipling Williams, and Stephen Harkins, "Many Hands Make Light the Work: The Causes and Consequences of Social Loafing," *Journal of Personality and Social Psychology* 37, no. 6 (June 1979): 822–832, https://doi.org/10.1037/0022-3514.337.6.822.

14. Create with Care

219 *lululemon's growth*: Lululemon Athletica Inc., "Lululemon Athletica Inc. Announces Fourth Quarter and Full Year Fiscal 2018 Results," press release, March 27, 2019, https://corporate.lululemon.com/media/press-releases/2019/03-27-2019-085957305; "Lululemon Revenue 2008–2023," Statista, January 14, 2025, https://www.statista.com/statistics/291238/net-revenue-of-lululemon-worldwide/.

228 *When Apple designed AirPods*: Jon Wilde, "Why Apple AirPods Came to Be Everywhere," *GQ*, March 22, 2019, https://www.gq.com/story/apple-airpods-everywhere.

228 *Zappos chose to remove time limits*: Joseph A. Michelli, *The Zappos Experience: 5 Principles to Inspire, Engage, and Wow* (McGraw Hill, 2011), 4.

Glossary

Apathy Chain: The fifth chain of change, measured at the individual level, manifesting as disengagement due to burnout, change fatigue, or frustration with constantly shifting priorities.

Change Fatigue: The physical, mental, and emotional exhaustion that occurs when people are subjected to too many organizational changes too quickly without sufficient support or purpose.

Chains of Change: The five fundamental barriers that keep organizations trapped in their comfort zones, unable to embrace transformation.

Clutter and Chaos Chain: The first chain of change, measured at the organizational level, where multiple competing priorities and constantly changing directions prevent effective progress.

Comfort with the Status Quo Chain: The second chain of change, measured at the individual level, where personal attachment to current systems and processes creates resistance to change.

Competing Interests Chain: The third chain of change, measured at both organizational and team levels, where different departments have conflicting goals and metrics.

Cone of Possibilities: A framework used to explore multiple futures beyond binary thinking, including possible futures (what could happen), plausible futures (what might happen), probable futures (what's likely to happen), and preferred futures (what should happen).

Constraints Chain: The fourth chain of change, measured at the organizational level, encompassing limitations in financial resources, time, talent, and competency.

Cocreation: The collaborative development of new value (concepts, solutions, products, services) together with experts and/or stakeholders rather than on their behalf.

Differentiation: Creating meaningful distinction from competitors through unique value proposition rather than incremental improvements to standard offerings.

Disruption: A transformation or dramatic change in how an industry functions, typically involving new technologies, business models, or approaches that displace established market leaders.

Innovation Principle: A fundamental guideline that directs transformative thinking and action, requiring specific mindset shifts to break free from chains of change.

Lagging Indicators: Metrics that measure past performance, expressing what has already happened (e.g., revenue, customer satisfaction scores, attendance rates).

Leading Indicators: Metrics that predict future performance, helping anticipate what might happen (e.g., voluntary contributions, spontaneous collaboration, innovation submissions).

Milli Mentors: The concept that instead of a single mentor, professionals benefit from a thousand diverse mentors providing situation-specific guidance at different points in their careers.

Social Loafing: The psychological phenomenon where individuals exert less effort when working in a large group than when working in small teams or alone, often occurring in large teams.

Spider Organizations: Centralized entities dependent on key leaders, where decision-making flows from the top down, making them vulnerable when those leaders leave.

Starfish Organizations: Decentralized networks built on contribution rather than control, where every part can function independently while serving the whole.

Strategic Sacrifice: The deliberate elimination of good options in service of great ones, creating focus that drives meaningful differentiation.

Total Addressable Market (TAM): The total market demand for a product or service, representing the upper limit of the potential market size a business can target.

Two-Way Door Decisions: Reversible choices that can be undone if they don't work out, contrasted with one-way door decisions that are difficult or impossible to reverse.

Tyranny of the Urgent: A state where everything feels like an emergency demanding immediate attention, preventing strategic thinking and causing teams to react rather than respond thoughtfully.

Work in Wonder: The practice of embracing curiosity instead of demanding certainty, using questions like "What if…" and "How might we…" to explore possibilities beyond current limitations.

About the Author

JAY KIEW IS the world's leading Change Fluency™ expert and a keynote speaker, with more than fifteen years of innovation experience, creating over $2 billion of impact for more than four hundred executives through organizational transformation. His groundbreaking Change Fluency model has revolutionized how organizations navigate complexity and change by driving growth through innovation. A half-blind cancer survivor, Jay exemplifies resilience in the face of adversity, equipping leaders to navigate change with both professional expertise and personal insight. The world's youngest Distinguished Toastmaster at age nineteen, Jay has been featured in *USA Today, Forbes, Business Insider, Financial Times, The Globe and Mail, Financial Post,* and *Ivey Business Journal,* and he was inducted as a Project Management Institute Future50 honoree in 2024 for his work on AI enablement. In 2025, Jay became a Canadian delegate for the G20 YEA Summit, advising on entrepreneurial policy regarding innovation, digitization, and the future of work. Jay holds an MBA from the Ivey Business School and lives in Vancouver with his wife, two daughters, and a stubborn Shiba Inu named Brooklyn.

JOIN THE TRANSFORMATION JOURNEY

Finding your path through disruption isn't about having all the answers—it's about asking better questions. I created the Change Fluency™ framework to be your companion as you navigate the complexities of leading change and driving innovation in a rapidly evolving world.

Connect with Me

Get deeper insights The journey doesn't end with the last page. Visit **changefluency.com/bookresources** for exclusive resources, downloadable templates for all the innovation exercises, and expanded case studies.

Bring these principles to your organization Transform how your team approaches change with customized Change Fluency workshops based on the five Chains of Change and the nine Innovation Principles. Learn more at **changefluency.com**.

Listen to conversations that matter Join me on The Change Fluency™ podcast where I interview transformation leaders who've successfully navigated disruption across industries. Subscribe at your favorite platform or visit **changefluency.com/change-fluency-podcast**.

Share Your Story

- Has *Change Fluency* helped you break a chain of change in your organization? I'd love to hear about it at **stories@changefluency.com**.

- Connect with fellow change champions by sharing your insights using **#ChampionChange** on social media.

- If the book has helped your team, consider leaving a review to help others discover these transformation principles.

Transform Your Team

Bulk orders and team resources Equip your entire organization with the tools to champion change. Special discounts available for orders of ten or more books, along with companion discussion guides and implementation road maps. Contact **books@changefluency.com**.

Book a keynote or workshop Bring the innovation principles to life through an engaging keynote or hands-on workshop customized for your organization's specific challenges. Visit **changefluency.com/change-fluency-keynotes** to learn more.

Remember Disruption isn't just something to survive—it's an opportunity to differentiate. Your journey to becoming a transformation leader starts now.

#ChampionChange
#ChangeFluencyBook

www.ingramcontent.com/pod-product-compliance
Lightning Source LLC
Chambersburg PA
CBHW031845200326
41597CB00012B/274